JOBSWORTH

JOBSWORTH

Confessions of the Man from the Council

Malcolm Philips

CHAPLIN BOOKS

www.chaplinbooks.co.uk

First published in 2013 by Chaplin Books
Copyright © Malcolm Philips

ISBN 978-1-909183-15-5

A CIP catalogue record for this book is available from The British Library

Design by Michael Walsh at The Better Book Company
Printed in the UK by Imprint Digital

Photography: Suprijoto Suharjoto/Dreamstime (front cover and frontispiece), Patrick Miller (back cover), Mammoth (pp iv,4,36,138,158), Borthwick Institute (p58), Cyberzoo (p60), Wallz (p81), Volkszone (p88), Ian Wilkes (p91), Wallpaperswide (p94), Dreamstime (p110), Damon Hart-Davis (p140). All other photographs by Amanda Field.

Chaplin Books
1 Eliza Place
Gosport PO12 4UN
Tel: 023 9252 9020
www.chaplinbooks.co.uk

CONTENTS

DEDICATION

I began these Confessions as a result of a pleasant yarning session over dinner with an old friend. We'd consumed one bottle of wine too many, and we fell to reminiscing about our working lives. I started recounting some of my experiences of working for local government in the 1960s and 1970s. My friend, God bless him, listened, claimed no boredom, occasionally chuckled, and was eventually kind enough to say "You ought to write these things down". So after a period of reflection, and several false starts, I did.

The more I wrote, the more the memories came forward. As I set the words down, and the cavalcade of people and events emerged from the past, I was surprised by the variety of the things that had touched me, particularly as life in the Council Offices might seem unpromising territory for characters and amusement. Distance in time may have added a little enchantment, or, indeed, disenchantment, to the view, some of the detail may not be absolute and in reality I might have been a little closer to or further away from the events I tell of, but believe me, everything I describe *did* happen, and the motley collection of jobsworths, crawlers, skivers, idealogues and thwarted good operators who added their own brands of spice or poison to my life and the lives of many others *did* exist. It is to those countless thwarted ones that I dedicate this book.

PROLOGUE

Ihave made few career choices in my life. In fact, at an age when many people have retired, I still don't really know what I want to do for a living.

One of the few solid choices I made happened at a pretty early age. I could read, so I must have been five or six at the time, and my choice was sparked by two notices in the local park. As with most parks, mine featured large areas of well-manicured grass which absolutely invited play. And yet much of this tempting space was adorned with stern notices which read 'Keep Off The Grass', a statement which made no sense to me at all. After all, the park was for the enjoyment of those who visited it. Wasn't it? The second notice stood by the park gates, and read 'These Gates Will Be Closed At 6.30pm. By Order'. Which again seemed just plain silly, particularly in summer when the light evenings might have allowed me to play outside until later than usual.

'Why?' I wailed to my parents, who said it was on the orders of the 'Local Council' who looked after the place and made the rules. I took an instant dislike to the 'Local Council'. I didn't know what it was, but I did know that I wanted nothing at all to do with it.

This youthful decision was reinforced when my father later became an employee of Middlesex County Council, and returned home from work almost every evening bemoaning the misery that the place caused him and the nastiness of the man who was his manager. The offices of Middlesex County Council were at that time, probably for some solid historical, but irrational, reason, situated in Great George Street in Westminster in a rather grand stone building, which had a central well to admit light into the offices facing inwards. My father had been allocated to the Education Department and worked in the school meals section, which, from my experience as a consumer of the product at the time, didn't seem likely to be a lot of fun. But perhaps there were times when it wasn't all gloom. I remember him telling us with some glee about looking out of his office across the well into a window on the floor below where the county educational psychologist, who was said to be – how shall we say? – somewhat eccentric, held court, and watching some of her antics. On one occasion a child was observed crawling around the floor with the psychologist crawling after it in hot pursuit, presumably trying to get in touch with the way it was thinking.

I was at an age when I still didn't really get the point of local government, and Father's tales didn't much help me to understand why it was there, either. I didn't know what I wanted to do for a living, except maybe engine driving or flying a jet plane, but one thing I was sure of was that I was never going to work for the council.

JOBSWORTH
Noun
British informal

An official who upholds petty rules even at the expense of humanity or common sense.

Example: 'parks abound with jobsworths who delight in yelling that you can't do that without special permission'

Origin: 1970s: from 'it's more than my job's worth (not) to'

1

ALL SODS AND BUGGERS

It all began in the late 1960s and though I was in my mid-twenties and had been working for some years, I still hadn't settled on what I actually wanted to do. No-one had offered me a job as a jet pilot or an engine driver, so I'd tried what turned out to be boring clerical work in a rather grim Thames Valley town, then moved to marginally less boring pen-pushing for a rather laid-back, paternalistic company in East Anglia. I'd then had the misplaced notion of 'going west' to become a professional photographer, and when that didn't work out, I had gravitated to a small printing company and then to a confectionery, ice cream and frozen food business.

Eventually I acquired the independence that a car gave, and was looking round, keen to explore new possibilities. After paying sterile visits to a number of businesses, I reluctantly turned my enquiries to the local county council, which lurked in an imposing, recently built headquarters a little out of the centre of the county town.

I turned up at County Hall one morning, and enquired of the uniformed man who finally emerged from hiding behind a pillar beside the front desk in the marble-clad entrance hall if there were any staff vacancies. That's how things were done in those days. He said that there probably were, made a phone call, and then directed me to the Establishment Office, a file-lined room staffed by two officers and a couple of clerical assistants. Looking back from an era in which 'HR' has donned the mantle of a profession, it seems unbelievable that an organisation employing around 15,000 people got by with just four people looking after the personnel matters for the entire workforce. I had already absorbed something of the unexciting feel of County Hall, and all the way to the office, I was praying that they would not have any vacancies and that I could go and look for a more interesting job somewhere else.

I was met by a time-served, kindly man called Keith Parsons, who told me there was no information available for prospective employees, so I'd just have to fill out an application form. (In fact, it wasn't until some time after I had joined the council, that a new establishment officer published a booklet for distribution at school careers conventions entitled 'So You Want to Be a Bureaucrat'. When I challenged this rather unappetising title, he was genuinely surprised. He seemed under the impression that 'Bureaucrat' was a word describing someone of great distinction).

Studying my completed form, Keith Parsons grunted and remarked that none of the experience I had gained in my career so far looked as if it might be useful in local government. Nevertheless, he checked for vacancies, and conceded that there might be a suitable clerical position in that part of the Education Department which dealt with school transport. Transport sounded good to me, so I said that I was interested, little realising that if I got the job I would not be dealing with major road and rail transport options for students, but simply keeping records of numbers and season tickets.

After a quick telephone call, Keith told me that I would need to be interviewed by the chief clerk of the Education Department, thus reinforcing my hopes that this might be a strategically important role. He escorted me to the chief clerk's office, knocked on the door, and after announcing my name thrust me in, and left. The chief clerk's name was Carter, and I later learned that he was universally referred to as 'Chiefer'. One of his distinguishing characteristics was that he carried out his conversations at the top of his voice.

"SIT DOWN!" shouted Chiefer. He spent a moment or two looking at my application form.

"HA. PHILIPS, EH? HAVEN'T WORKED FOR A COUNCIL, THEN? ONLY EXPERIENCE IN INDUSTRY. NOT SURE YOU'LL UNDERSTAND WORK HERE THEN, WILL YOU? EH? YES! RIGHT! HA, HA!"

Not only was the whole interview conducted at top volume, but the opportunities for me to reply to questions were non-existent.

"THERE'S A FEW DIFFICULT PEOPLE HERE, Y'KNOW," he yelled. "ALL SODS AND BUGGERS, HA, HA!"

I emerged from Chiefer's office after fifteen minutes or so, mentally reeling and shell-shocked, to find Keith leaning against the corridor wall outside with a faint grin on his face.

"How did you get on, then?" he said as we walked away. His voice seemed very quiet after Chiefer's aural bombardment.

I was silent for a moment or two, and then replied "I don't really know."

The grin became a little broader. "Do you know," he said, "I hate that man."

As we worked our way back to the calm of the Establishment Office, I was asking myself if I really wanted to work in this place. Keith must have read my mind, or been very used to the response of potential new recruits who'd had the same experience.

"There are a lot of different kinds of people here," he said quite gently. "If you're still interested, give me a ring tomorrow and let me know."

I returned home in a state of confusion and indecision. I talked things over with my parents, who had also moved to the west, and with whom I still lived. They were of little help. Father suggested that I might have a good solid career ahead of me if I joined the council, huffed a bit when I reminded him of his Middlesex experience, and claimed, with absolutely no proof I could detect, that things were different now. Mother said it was up to me, so she wasn't a lot of help, either. Views of friends from whom I sought advice were also unhelpful, and if they had anything to say at all their statements usually contained words like "boring" and "faceless".

After deliberating for a couple of days, I made the phone call, somewhat without conviction, and was told that I could start in a few weeks' time as a clerical assistant on the lowliest pay scale, which in those days was called 'Clerical 1 (Bar)'. I understood that the 'bar' was a salary point through which only those gifted with some kind of god-like excellence could progress.

The die was cast. I was, reluctantly, a fully signed-up trainee jobsworth, ready to encounter the sods and buggers who inhabited County Hall.

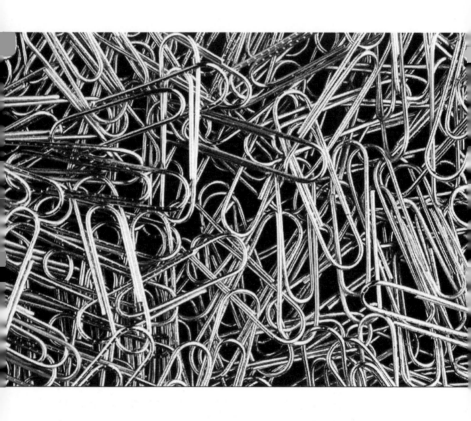

2

THE WRONG CHAIR

On the day which might have marked the beginning of my eventual elevation to greatness, Father wished me well and just as I was leaving home Mother thrust a pack of sandwiches at me ("You never know what the canteen arrangements might be"). It was a bit like my first day at school.

I drove to my new life at County Hall in my 1955 Austin Somerset saloon, which had bench seats, column gear change and trafficators, those little orange-coloured pointers indicating an intention to turn that shot out from the side of the car when you pressed the lever. The car had originally been a fawn colour, which had weathered over the years to a pinkish hue, and its registration was SOW 211. It was a vehicle of uncertain habits, which blew head gaskets every 6,000 miles or so, and had something of an appetite for new front shock absorbers. It behaved well that day, however, and I tentatively selected a place in the County Hall car-park which seemed as if it would cause no offence to other established users.

I had arrived in good time, so I sat tight for a few minutes, frozen with stage-fright, watching the flood of apparently eager employees climbing the steps to the main entrance and disappearing into the interior like a multitude of Jonahs being swallowed by the whale, or perhaps like lemmings heading towards an unavoidable cliff edge. Eventually I gathered my courage, straightened my tie and joined the throng.

I reported to the reception desk, where the same uniformed commissionaire was still hiding behind his pillar, hoping to avoid as many visitors as possible. After hovering for a while, I finally made my presence felt, and was told that I would have to wait for the appointed hour. When I finally found my way to the Establishment Office, Keith informed me that plans had changed – I had been drafted not to Education, but to the Health Department instead. Even in those days, when the NHS was nearly 20 years old, county authorities continued to be responsible for a whole range of health services, from district nurses and the ambulance service, to school health and dentistry.

Keith escorted me to the office which for the next year or so would be my workplace. The section head and his second-in-command were absent – they were at what was colloquially known as 'morning prayers', the ritual daily post-opening ceremony in the mailroom (clearly, one had to be pretty high up to be involved in this). I was introduced, therefore, to the most senior person left in the office, Archie.

Archie was middle-aged and lean, with a corpse-like pallor. He was also one of those people who seem to come to work as a penance, in order to have a bad day. Like all such, his expectations of a bad day were generally fulfilled, and this was reflected in his demeanour and approach to life. His major task was the processing of travel claims for those in the Department who were designated 'travelling officers'. His work was thorough and accurate, his handwriting neat and his records perfectly filed. He was an inveterate smoker of Player's No. 6 cigarettes, and was renowned for his use of bad language, which became obvious right away. His opening words to me after Keith had gone and the formal "How do you do's?" had been said, were "What the bloody hell have come to this bloody place for?"

He showed me around the various offices, and introduced me to everyone, so my first half-hour became a confusing sea of faces and an information-overload of detail about what jobs the faces did. I can remember only one of the introductions from Archie, and that was when he ushered me into the presence of a gentle, middle-aged, owl-like man who worked part-time in our office and part-time somewhere else.

"This 'ere is Willie. He's an idle bugger because he's only here half the time."

I later found Archie to be a generous man with a heart of gold, and an interesting sense of humour. When he first saw the colour of my car he remarked that it was very like that of a pig, and matched the registration to a tee. From then on he was wont to ask, "How's the old SOW, then?" I'd told him that the car was always giving me trouble, and I also think he'd figured out that I was having girlfriend problems, so whenever he asked about the SOW, I was never sure to which of my life's tribulations he was referring.

Archie had a reputation for being tetchy, and had a number of rigidly fixed ideas. His attitude was the source of some amusement among his colleagues. In his private life he was a Special Constable, and on most Mondays he entertained us with satisfied tales of weekend law enforcement. Some of his tetchiness may have had its roots in his war service, much of which was spent in Italy, and I believe he had been in the battle for Monte Cassino. He had lost part of a foot in action, and had spent time in an Italian hospital. From time to time he regaled us with the story of how the Pope came to visit those in the hospital. When we asked how he knew who the visitor was, he was adamant that it *was* the Pope, and that, moreover, he had had his wife with him, so that proved it!

Archie went home to lunch every day, and it was a point of honour with him that he always left the office five minutes early. At five minutes to one he would put down his pen, light up a No. 6, and get his mac from the coat hook. Every day the timing was exact and the process identical and woe betide anyone who attempted to interfere. One day, just as Archie was rising from his chair, the departmental deputy chief came into the office with a travel claim form. The deputy was a quiet man and – like many – didn't really know how to handle Archie.

"Er, Archie," he said tentatively, holding his form up like a piece of damp washing on a line. "Archie, I wonder if you can push this one through quickly for me. I'm a bit short this month."

Archie finished lighting his cigarette, looked the deputy straight in the eye and replied "You can go and have a ferking good shite, mate. I'm going to lunch." He put on his mac, gave me a broad wink, and left.

The deputy didn't really know what to do. "I'll leave it here then," he said, placing the form carefully on Archie's desk, and leaving the room quietly.

After the confusion of the introductions, Ron, who was the section head, and Paul, his second in command, appeared fresh from morning prayers bearing a mountain of mail, which was handy because it transpired that my job depended on what was in the post. Paul instructed me in my work, which turned out to be the boring, useless kind of clerical activity that I was dreading. I had two tiers of card trays on trolleys, a desk, a chair, an 'IN' tray and an 'OUT' tray. All the invoices which arrived from suppliers were distributed to those giants who were allowed to be in charge of official order books. They tore out the second copy of the official order, stapled it to the invoice, and stuck a 'coding slip' to the invoice. The coding slip had space for two signatures, the first of which was that of the order-book holder who confirmed that the goods or services had been delivered, and the second was provided by an even more exalted person who confirmed that the whole thing was upright and legal, and conformed to financial regulations, and that, basically, the first signatory wasn't telling fibs.

My job came between the first and second signature. The first signatory passed the papers to me, and I had to fill in a seven- or sometimes ten-digit coding number on the slip. It was not explained to me what purpose this served, but I eventually discovered that it meant that the cost was allocated to the right part of the budget. I then filled in details of the invoice on the appropriate supplier record card in my stack, together with the date it was passed for payment. Having done this, I then passed the pile of papers to the second signatory. And that was that. Quite why the job existed I don't know, because the whole process could have been completed in a much more effective way. But, being a newly installed jobsworth, I never questioned the why and the how.

Mother was right to query the lunch arrangements. I later found out that there was a staff club which served passable lunches, but no-one had thought to mention it and it was many months before I risked going there: in the meantime I ate sandwiches in the office. This provision of a staff club, which was financially self-supporting, was very much a reflection of the times. Not only did it provide a canteen for those who worked at County Hall, but it also had a more classy restaurant with silver service for the councillors. There was a lounge area with a television, a few games facilities and a fully licensed bar, open at lunchtimes and in the evening, available for all those connected with the Council. For many, a pint and a pasty was a pleasurable alternative to the canteen or a pack of sandwiches from home. Occasionally, multiple pints were consumed and although gross incapability seldom resulted, it was a given that in one or two departments, getting much sense out of some of them on a Friday afternoon was not always possible.

When I returned home from my first day's labours, Father asked me how I had got on.

"It went OK," I said, non-committal.

"What was the work like?" he asked.

I shrugged. "My first job after I left school was more challenging than this."

"Never mind," he said. "Stick with it and show them how good you are."

Unfortunately, though, the job didn't give too many opportunities to show how good I was. I soon discovered that on most days that I could be through with the work by lunchtime, and, on some days, by ten o'clock. It was a sinecure. Boring and, on the face of it, pretty pointless, but a sinecure, nonetheless. But there was one major advantage: the spare time could always be spent in wandering about and socialising, which inevitably included chatting up female members of staff.

Occasionally I had to send out standard letters to suppliers requesting more information. I was not allowed to sign my own name on these letters, and the process introduced me to the quaint habit, which still exists today in some dark corners of some local authorities, of having to sign the name of the chief. I often wondered about the validity of what was, after all, a forged signature.

There were one or two other rules and traditions which I had to learn.

Tea of a somewhat questionable nature was wheeled around the department morning and afternoon by a tea lady. I was well used to this kind of system from previous jobs, but I had not been informed that here I was supposed to provide my own mug. On my first day I was offered the use of a spare mug retrieved from a window-sill, but I balked at the state of this cracked vessel with the mouldy remains of some substance stuck firmly in the bottom, and politely refused. So for the day of my entry I was tea-less.

By about day three I began to understand the hierarchical nature of furniture use in the authority. The lowlier the grade of the worker, the smaller was their desk, which didn't seem logical, because the lower-grade people often had more paperwork to deal with than their more senior colleagues. I had also noticed that there was a chair which looked more comfortable than mine standing unused in a corner of the office. Without thinking, I exchanged my green coloured chair without arms for the unused grey one, which had arms. Archie noticed this, and came over to me. In kindly tones he informed me that I was now sitting on the wrong ferking kind of chair.

"On your grade," quoth he, "you should have the green chair. The grey one is for people on Senior Officer Grade and above." The comfortable chair was left once again to play out its empty life in the corner.

One of the more interesting parts of my duties was the delivery of invoices for the second signature. At first I had asked Archie where the people sat, but his usual response was a sigh followed by "Didn't you pay any ferking attention when I showed you around on your first day?" so I soon learned the geography for myself by trial and error. The latter was usually indicated by someone dumping some papers back on my desk grunting "This is nothing to do with me".

The Department had two typing rooms, one at each end of the corridor. These were occupied by a group of women, one or two rather fanciable, each room being watched over by a senior typist. One of the seniors was a charming and kindly country woman, all jam and Jerusalem, who apparently had no problem in allowing me into her domain to pass the time of day with some of her staff. The other room was ruled over by a straightlaced spinster of fierce countenance with piercing eyes which bored through any visitor to her kingdom, and who would not let me past her desk.

These rooms, which were sometimes called 'typing pools', and their occupants – banks of women (and they were all women in those days) – tapping, and, sometimes, if their machines were elderly or ill-disposed to them, hammering, away on typewriter keyboards, are now consigned to history. Although there were an increasing number of electric typewriters around, many manual specimens still existed. Our two rooms were territories where, because of the sound effects, there was always an impression of busy activity and important documents being produced.

The room lorded over by the straitlaced spinster was also home to the County Medical Officer's secretary, Dorothy Lin, a delightful and efficient woman of Chinese extraction, always turned out immaculately and with impeccable bearing, who was everybody's notion of the ideal personal assistant. She was polite and respectful of everyone, and was a great favourite of all; perhaps one of her greatest assets was that she was one of the few people who could handle Archie with ease. When from time to time he had overstretched the mark, and she had to summon him to a chat with the chief, which many would have found uncomfortable, he was as putty in her hands.

For a brief time, a rather wacky occasional girlfriend of mine was also an occupant. In a way, I was responsible for her getting a job with the council. Miss Wacky, whose real name was emphatically double-barrelled with a voice and demeanour to match, had parents who had retired to the county, and after a time she had abandoned a life in London to join them. During an early social conversation with her she'd moaned that there didn't seem to be much in the way of decent secretarial work around, and I had suggested, almost without thinking, that she might try her luck at County Hall. I was surprised when she told me she would, because I had already formed the view that life in our backwater was hardly likely to satisfy her desire for the sort of dynamic and exciting life she had apparently enjoyed in London.

While on a shopping trip to the county town Miss Wacky had visited a pet shop where, on impulse, she'd bought a tortoise. After this, again on impulse, she had made her way to County Hall to see about possible jobs. It was only when she reached the reception desk that she remembered she was carting around the cardboard box containing the tortoise. Using her best commanding tones, she attracted the attention of the earlier-mentioned uniformed commissionaire, who reluctantly emerged from his hiding place and enquired if she needed help.

"I've come to offer my services to the council as a senior secretary," she pronounced, making it quite clear by implication that she was doing the organisation a great favour. After establishing that she had no appointment, the uniformed one phoned the Establishment Office and she was summoned for an immediate interview. She was worldly-wise enough to appreciate that clutching a box containing a tortoise while talking about possible employment to an unknown representative of an organisation of which she knew little might not be very impressive, so she asked the commissionaire to look after the tortoise. His reply was, so she later told me, something like "Look after your own sodding tortoise", but he did melt a little, and secreted the box on a shelf under the desk.

Miss Wacky was delighted to emerge later from the Establishment Office with a job offer, and marched in a business-like manner towards the main entrance of the building, to which a good number of employees were also heading, it being close to going-home time.

"Goodnight," she carolled, slightly condescendingly, to the commissionaire.

"'Ere, miss, don't forget your blinking tortoise!"

Thus she became something of a legend even before she started work with us.

Predictably, her tenure as a county employee didn't last long. She got bored, and some of her approaches to working life didn't mesh too well with the way things were done in local government. She decided to return to the supposed sophistication of the capital after a few months, but not before she had made a bid for a different kind of adventure. Although not Jewish herself, along with many people at the time she sympathised with the Israeli cause which led to the six-day war of June 1967. Immediately the brief campaign began, she telephoned the Israeli embassy to offer her services and was highly put out when they politely, but firmly, turned her offer down. Some of her colleagues thought that she was a bit barmy, but given the time for reflection offered by the passing years, I still think that 'Wacky' is the best description.

The second typing room had a much more relaxed atmosphere than the first, and this stemmed from the style of the supervisor. It also had a larger number of attractive occupants, but I remember it as well because presence of one of the more mature typists. She was known by all as Miss Jury, and was never referred to by her Christian name. In fact, I doubt whether many actually knew what her Christian name was. She had been a virtuous and reliable employee for many years, and was wedded to her manual machine; nothing would persuade her to use an electric typewriter. Her typing, though, was always immaculate, and for that reason she was often given prestige jobs where total accuracy and quality of layout were paramount. She seemed proud and happy with her role, and apparently wanted little more in life. Her approach to work made her almost a paragon of virtue. In fact, it seemed as if life at County Hall provided her with all that she needed. She was a quiet and unobtrusive person who seemed to spend much of her time on a planet of her own. She lived alone in her own house, probably with a cat, and had a small, clean car which brought her to work in good time every day. In fact her addiction to the quality of life offered by her job was demonstrated on at least a couple of occasions, when well-established habit and routine meant that without thinking she arrived promptly for work, and only realised that it was Sunday when she found the car park empty and the entrances locked. She was surely a committed servant of the council.

One office in the Health Department was the domain of a section called Child Health which among other duties was responsible for storing and distributing vaccines for the usual childhood inoculations. The vaccines were stored in a large freezer and refrigerator in one corner of the office. As the year progressed into summer, I learned that the staff in the section put ice-cream in the same freezer, and I wondered what kind of epidemic might have been set in motion if by any chance one of the vials of vaccine ruptured and leaked its contents on to the ice-cream cartons. Summer also brought about a curious ceremony carried out by the section head, a taciturn man who possessed an immaculate Armstrong Siddeley saloon car. The car was always placed in the car park in such a position that one side was protected from the sun, and at some point on sunny days the proud owner would leave his post to cover the tyres of the vehicle on the unshaded side with old coats kept in the boot for this purpose. Something to do with protecting the rubber from harmful rays, I was told.

The county nursing officer had her own office. She was a formidable woman of the old-fashioned matron school. She was always direct and courteous with any queries I had, but I was glad that I never got on the wrong side of her. She had a large picture of Queen Victoria on the wall, and it seemed probable that Her Majesty was the nursing officer's role model.

Another office housed the admin people for the district nursing and health visitor service. A major part of one clerk's duties was producing records relating to midwifery, all of which were duly submitted to the county medical officer and then to the Health Committee. They formed one of those papers in committee bundles which no-one actually uses, but which everyone assumes is informative and of use to someone else. Later it was discovered that these particular records had been produced since somewhere around the end of World War I, when the then county medical officer asked the committee to approve the appointment of two extra midwives. The committee had apparently asked him to produce evidence to support his case: when he did so, he duly got his extra staff. The only problem was that no-one ever stopped the paper being produced, and for years a string of clerical assistants had diligently continued the production of a document which served no purpose whatsoever.

The curiosities of the way in which some clerical work was handled also occurred elsewhere in this section at the hands of the section head, a middle-aged man. Every district nurse, midwife and health visitor was entitled to an annual issue of uniform. Their needs were submitted on a form, and the contents of the forms were collated to make up orders to be sent to suppliers. This was a perfectly straightforward clerical operation which could have been done anywhere by any junior clerk. Every year, however, the section head insisted on undertaking the job himself. One or two of us had unworthy suspicions about the motives which required him to delve so deeply into the business of women's measurements and needs ...

Archie had some interesting dealings with the district nurses and health visitors regarding their travel expense claims. Approached in the right way, he bent over backwards to help solve their queries or answer their questions, usually over the phone. With one or two of the more forthright and demanding kind, however, he was in a state of armed truce which sometimes used to flare up into open warfare. A classic, which we treasured, was when, after a long patient and rational conversation with a particularly persistent district nurse who still did not understand what he had told her several times, a flare occurred. He told her to "Ferk off" and hung up the phone. Within minutes Dorothy, the county medical officer's impeccable secretary appeared, and summoned Archie into the presence of the chief. He responded to her bidding as he usually did, and followed her like a lamb. Some form of vaguely disciplinary conversation with the chief ensued, but a grinning Archie returned, unscathed and unapologetic, to light another No. 6 and continue with his day.

Archie also used to keep mileage records. On one occasion he chatted to a district nurse who had been issued with a new Morris Minor about the fact that the petrol consumption was much more than might be expected. It transpired that the nurse's previous vehicle had had a three-speed gearbox, and she had not realised that the new car had four gears: she had been travelling everywhere in third. Another time, when he requested information about a minor collision which had occurred when another nurse was leaving her driveway, she told him disdainfully that she couldn't understand why the other car had hit her. "Everybody round here knows that I leave for work at that time," she said. Mind, nurses and health visitors were not the only ones Archie engaged with. There was one splendid altercation with an occupational therapist who had driven into her garage forgetting that the car's roof rack was piled high with the tools and materials of her trade, thus writing off the tools and materials, the roof rack and the car. Small wonder, perhaps, that Archie sometimes put his telephone down at the end of a conversation shaking his head sadly, and muttering "Scatty as a box of arseholes!"

The people at the top of the hierarchy were remote, especially from those as humble as me. I only visited the chief medical officer's palatial territory once and I can't even remember why. I recall there was some nice hardwood panelling to waist level, as was usual in all chiefs' offices, some classy-looking watercolours adorning the walls, the usual adherence to the protocols governing the size of the desk, and additionally, again as in all chiefs' lairs, an impressive table which formed the centrepiece for important meetings. There was a deputy chief and a couple of other fully-fledged doctors whose purpose in life remained a mystery to me, although one of them, a woman, seemed much involved with the selection of curtain materials for Health Centres.

Every few weeks the Health Committee met, and all the top management and section heads appeared smartly turned out in what we *hoi polloi* referred to as their 'committee suits'. All except, that is, the county ambulance officer, who attended attired in a uniform with a lot of silver braid. Interesting, this, because I believe that professional ambulance work was not something that he had ever been connected with. His deputy was an ex-police sergeant who seemed to miss the structure and discipline of the police force very much. He also had a uniform (with slightly less silver braid) which he wore as often as possible while on official duties, probably to remind him of old times.

A perk – at least I thought it was one – attached to my job was the occasional excursion into milk testing. Every day inspectors travelled the county visiting dairy farms and collecting milk samples, which were then delivered to the Health Department to test for brucellosis, which I learned was bovine tuberculosis. The samples were normally dealt with by Don, a small man who grunted and sniffed a great deal, and whose main task aside from testing milk samples was collecting the post from various offices. Don had a little laboratory in the basement of the building and disappeared into this mid-morning, not emerging again until post collection time in the afternoon. If any of the samples tested positive he would put them on the carrier on his bike and ride into the city centre to deliver them to an organisation called 'The Public Analyst' for further more detailed testing. The bike was kept in the basement, and I can remember all hell, accompanied by a good deal of grunting and sniffing, being let loose when someone hid it in an adjacent storeroom. From then on the machine was tethered by lock and chain to the banisters on the stairs.

When Don was away, I deputised. I can't remember the exact routine, but I do recall that hydrochloric acid and a centrifuge played a significant part in the process. I never had many positive samples but when I did, the trip to the public analyst was a pleasant diversion. Situated in a converted house in a Georgian terrace, the laboratory was like something out of Victorian England. Wooden fume-cupboards adorned the stained walls and Bunsen burners abounded, and there was always a curious smell, compounded from chemicals and gas.

Don got quite ratty with me because I dealt with the milk samples reasonably quickly, and he was afraid that his disappearance for a long period every day might be curtailed if those in charge noticed that the job could be done more rapidly.

My first summer in local government was spent being bored by the work, in much socialising in various offices (we had a noughts and crosses league in one), looking out at the heat-haze over the distant hills, and watching for the sight of one of our typists, Julie, climbing out of her Mini in the car park. The Mini in question was a car, but Julie was also the first exponent of the mini skirt at County Hall, and very nice she was, too.

On hot days I felt envious of those who could travel around on county business. There was a rule which allowed those who travelled to claim a subsistence allowance for lunch, provided that they were visiting somewhere three or more miles away and that they left their normal workplace before 11.30am. I was never quite able to see the sense of this (although that did not stop me claiming my allowance when I became an official traveller on county business) because people had to buy their lunch in some form or another wherever they were. At about 11.20am Archie, whose desk was by the window, would intone "It's a nice sunny day. Let's go out and measure something!" and we would watch the procession of important, and sometimes not so important, people laden with briefcases and files and rolls of plans wending their ways to their cars. There were highways works to be visited, schools to check out, planning site meetings to be attended and a hundred and one other reasons for travelling to take place. The population of County Hall diminished remarkably when the weather was right. One red-letter day we watched with glee as a very senior officer put his briefcase on the top of his car while he stowed other items on the back seat, forgot that it was there and drove off with the briefcase sitting neatly on the roof. We speculated how far it might travel in this way.

"Doesn't really matter," said Archie with some satisfaction, "He's probably only got his sandwiches in the briefcase. That means if it falls off he'll have to spend his ferking lunch allowance on lunch!"

Ron, the section head, came over to my desk one day in the summer. "Thought I'd let you know that you are going up to the college of further education in September," he said. This came as something of a surprise.

"What for?" I asked.

"To do the Diploma in Public Administration," answered Ron. "Day release, every Wednesday. The Council's paying."

"Why me?"

"Well," said Ron, patiently, "We always send one person from this Department, and it's your turn."

I am all for personal development, but this decision has always seemed to me a prime example of untargeted training. It was, however, clearly useless to argue, so in September I exchanged a day of tedium at work for an alternative sort of academic tedium at the college. Administrative Law was delivered by a solicitor whose idea of tuition was the constant dictation of notes, which among other things, enabled us to learn about snails in ginger beer bottles and horse buses which turned over while racing, but little of it seemed to be relevant to local government. Structure of Government Bodies was presented by a college lecturer who seemed proud of the fact, which he shared with us several times, that he could not visit the United States because he had once been a card-carrying member of the Communist party. His enthusiasm for such obscure organisations as the Tomato Marketing Board was unbounded, but I couldn't share his excitement. Economics was delivered by a dogmatic middle-aged woman who would brook little argument and who took few prisoners, and there was also something about the parliamentary system, and a revisit to an 'O' Level approach to English. I managed to drop out after a few months.

Gradually I fell into the ways of public service. Unhurried, structured, solid, unexciting. One of the more interesting events when the Health Department had to undergo an organisation and methods review. Organisation and Methods – usually referred to as 'O&M' – was new to me. It is, nowadays, almost a lost art, but in those days every public service body, and many commercial businesses, too, had an O&M Department. Their task was to examine the work that people did in the organisation with a view to finding more effective ways of operating. Members of staff were interviewed and encouraged to talk about the processes of their jobs, and the O&M team then compiled a report. As might be imagined, O&M people were not universally loved, because they often suggested changes in work practices and sometimes even recommended eliminating certain things altogether. I talked at length with the young man who interviewed me, quite liking the sound of O&M, and started to wonder vaguely how I might become a practitioner.

A landmark activity for the whole council that summer was the installation of the first mainframe computer. We had a grandstand view of all the bits and pieces being unloaded in the car park, and some of the building alterations which took place. The machine started to operate in the autumn, churning out employees' payslips and cheques for creditors. In our slightly sleepy hollow we noticed little change, though.

One of the things that differed from the ways in which my previous employers had operated was the fact that most vacancies were advertised internally. Late in the year, a vacancy for a trainee computer systems analyst appeared. Aside from the fact that the salary grade was higher than my meagre Clerical Grade 1 (Bar), the notion of research and systems development appealed to me, and I applied. A number of my colleagues told me I didn't have a chance, mainly because the new post was paid on the Administrative and Professional Grade 2 and 3, and it was unusual for anyone to gravitate to these dizzy heights from the basic clerical grade.

I got an interview!

The interviewers were the county management services officer and the chief systems analyst. The former had a reputation for being fierce and remote. I wasn't sure how the interview was going, but I got a bit of a clue when Fierce and Remote waved his hand in the direction of my application form and said "You've changed jobs and moved around quite often. How long are you going to stay here?"

Without thinking I replied, "I'll stay here as long as there's something here for me."

When Fierce and Remote looked at me and said "That's a good answer", I felt that I might just be getting somewhere. In due course I was thanked for my attendance, and left feeling reasonably confident.

Within a week an internal letter informed me that I had been unsuccessful. I wasn't too downcast, but I would have liked a different result. Anyway, my colleagues' opinions had been vindicated.

Three weeks or so later, I was surprised to be summoned into the presence of the two interviewers again. Fierce and Remote, never a man to beat about the bush, got straight to the point.

"Are you still interested in the trainee systems analyst post?"

"Yes, sir."

"The person we offered the job to has withdrawn, so we are offering it to you. However, we don't know much about you so we'll be appointing you on the lower AP1 grade, to be reviewed after six months."

I was delighted, and it didn't strike me until much later that they hadn't known much about the bloke who had withdrawn, either, and yet he was still offered the full whack!

3

FLOWER POWER IN THE COMPUTER ROOM

The council's computer installation was considered to be
state of the art. The mainframe sat in the middle of a large,
especially converted, air-conditioned and temperature-
controlled room. Smoking was forbidden in the room and the area
surrounding it. Data was entered into the computer on punched
cards, each of the card's 80 columns representing a number from
0 to 10, or an alphabetic character or a symbol. The information
on the cards was transferred into the machine by a noisy card
reader. There was a line printer – so called because it printed
one line of type at a time – for output, and the only keyboard in
sight (not a trace of a screen) was for control of the mainframe
and its peripherals. Our computer was reckoned superior because
information was stored on large discs, thus giving 'random
access' to data, which was impossible on the then more generally
used reel-to-reel tapes.

Surrounding the computer room were rooms for
programmers and operating staff. The computer manager, Rod,
had his own office with all-round windows, which was squeezed
between the programmers and data preparation. The business of
data preparation was undertaken by a large team of young women
who keyed in information from documents, such as invoices, on
machines which punched patterns of holes on to the 80-column
cards.

Rod, it was rumoured, had a bit of an eye for the ladies and
the data preparation team was frequently referred to as 'Rod's
harem'. Rod was a knowledgeable, if somewhat verbose man,
but although he had a liking for the opposite sex and seemed to
think that he was God's gift to women, his taciturn and frankly
unexciting demeanour might have prevented the occupants of any
harem from throwing themselves at him in adoration *en masse*.

"I'm not sure I'll ever get the hang of this computing stuff," I said as he walked me round his empire.

"The principles of computing are simple," said Rod. "Everything is based on logic. We only use 'ones' and 'zeros' – it's called binary – and our up-to-date kit uses hexadecimal, which is pretty sophisticated. You'll get to grips with it soon enough."

```
0 0 0   0 0 0 0   0   0 0 0 0 0 0 0 0 0 0 0 0 0 0
1 2 3  4 5 6 7  8  9 10 11 12 13 14 15 16 17 18 19 20 21 22 23 24 25 26
    1 1 1 1 1   1     1 1 1 1 1 1 1 1 1 1 1 1 1 1 1
2 2 2 2   2 2 2 2 2 2 2 2 2 2 2 2 2 2 2 2 2 2 2 2 2
3 3 3   3 3   3   3 3 3 3 3 3 3 3 3 3 3 3 3 3 3 3 3
4 4 4 4 4 4 4 4 4 4 4 4 4 4 4 4 4 4 4 4 4 4 4 4 4 4
5 5   5 5   5 5 5 5 5 5 5 5 5 5 5 5 5 5 5 5 5 5 5 5
6 6 6 6 6 6 6 6 6 6 6 6 6 6 6 6 6 6 6 6 6 6 6 6 6 6
7 7 7 7 7 7 7 7 7 7 7 7 7 7 7 7 7 7 7 7 7 7 7 7 7 7
8 8 8   8 8   8   8 8 8 8 8 8 8 8 8 8 8 8 8 8 8 8 8
1 2 3  4 5 6 7  8  9 10 11 12 13 14 15 16 17 18 19 20 21 22 23 24 25 26
9 9 9 9 9 9 9 9 9 9 9 9 9 9 9 9 9 9 9 9 9 9 9 9 9 9
```

Hexadecimal? It was beginning to sound even more daunting.

"Don't forget," he cautioned, "When you get round to writing your systems, don't use too much alphabetic information."

"Why not?"

"Because it takes up too much space in the machine."

The influx of 'computer types' had some interesting side-effects on the council's culture. Until their appearance, it was usual for all male employees to wear suits, and in the more staid departments, such as the Treasurer's or Education, dark suits were utterly the rule. Elsewhere sports jackets were just about just about allowable, as long as they were of dowdy colouring. Nobody would have dreamed of appearing in any other garb. Even garish ties were *de trop*: shirts had to be white, or with almost unnoticeable patterns. I spent most of my local authority life as a sports jacket man, and I suppose that this might have marked me out as having a tendency towards minor mutiny. But these computer people were from a new and hitherto unknown world and in their corner of the building there was a sudden rash of bright colours, flower power, sandals and kaftans, and even, God save us all, of sometimes no ties, not to mention pink shirts when these first appeared in gents' clothing departments. The only other class of person who indulged in sartorial rebellion, but on a much smaller scale, were planners, who were inclined to wear their shirts outside their trousers.

One senior and long-standing member of the Treasurer's department was heard to bemoan the clothing situation while looking out of his office window and viewing staff walking from the car park to the main entrance. "Look at them," he said. "Planners are bad enough, but look at those scruffy herberts of computer people. Local authority dignity's gone to the dogs!"

The female staff had their own fashion issues to wrestle with. When I first started at County Hall, generally sober if sometimes fashionable, feminine attire was the norm, but this was shattered by the emergence of the mini-skirt. Some male old-stagers, goodness knows why, tried to move heaven and earth to have them ruled out of order, but, mercifully, they were unsuccessful. Later, towards the mid-seventies, female staff made repeated calls for women to be allowed to wear trousers. I seem to remember that their cause was greatly helped by the chill of Edward Heath's three-day week.

The notion of using computing for anything other than jobs dealing with numbers was still relatively new, but there was a dawning appreciation of the wider possibilities. Perhaps it was with this in mind that the council had decided to split the responsibility between the Treasurer's Department, who were responsible for operations and programming, and the Management Services Department, who designed the inputs and outputs for systems, and installed them in user departments. This division between the people who designed the systems and the programmers that implemented them was not always common, but was intended to ensure that users were not simply at the mercy of the technical experts. "You can't let those clever programmers loose on the users of the systems," the senior systems analyst, my manager, told me. "They'd simply confuse everybody and invent paperwork that no-one could understand." All this meant that I was to sit in the Management Services Department as one of the handful of people who tried to make sure that the systems were user-friendly and did what users wanted them to do.

After only a few days, I was sent on a four-week course at the Royal Institute of Public Administration in London. The course was called 'An Introduction to O&M' and when I queried this with the chief systems analyst he told me that it would help me understand fact-finding, systems design and installation. So perhaps my previous interest in O&M might be bearing fruit after all.

The Royal Institute of Public Administration occupied part of a Regency terrace in a crescent near Regent's Park. There were about twenty of us, mainly from local authorities, on the course and it was an interesting time. Much of the interest centred on a couple of members of the Institute's secretarial staff – Australians who lived in that part of Earls Court, which was in those days colloquially known as 'kangaroo alley'. In addition to visits to kangaroo alley, a small gang of us had a beer or two and walked around the West End after the course day had finished.

There was one pleasant chap on the course who was a very serious character, and who seemed a bit of a loner. I think he worked for a local authority administering one of the less picturesque parts of South Yorkshire. We were determined that he shouldn't leave London without having his experience of life broadened, so in the final week we persuaded him to come out with us after the course had finished for the day, and walked him through Soho. After all, this was 1968; London was swinging and not too far away from where we were was Carnaby Street, the centre of fashion. In a pub, we had beer, and he had orange juice. Afterwards, we paused outside Raymond's Review Bar.

"Just look at these photographs," I said, indicating the exotic pictures of girls that adorned the entrance to the nightclub.

He took a perfunctory look, stepped back, and gazed up at the building. "By gum," he said, "I bet the rateable value of this place is something."

We gave up at this point, walked with him back to his hotel and went our various ways.

Back at County Hall, I received my first commission, which was to write a system for shotgun registration. The government had decreed that shotguns must be registered in a similar, but slightly less complicated way, to other firearms. They had apparently carried out their research in the Metropolitan Police area, where there may have been shedloads of shotguns, but only a few people who owned up to possessing one. In the manner of governments, they therefore assumed that all other police forces would find it to be an easy system to apply. Our constabulary policed a very large rural area, and when the applications for licences started to appear it was obvious that their number would run into tens of thousands. The decision to use the computer was a very sensible one.

I made many journeys to the police headquarters to meet the people who would use the system, and to view the documents involved. The application form was relatively simple and caused me no problem in terms of designing the format in which it could be entered into the computer. My system did not include the section which asked about previous convictions, because dodgy ones were weeded out by the police before they were sent on to us, but I did enjoy odd moments of reading about minor offences. I remember one farmer who solemnly confessed on his application that he was "fined 10/- in 1932 for driving a traction engine without a spark arrester".

One of the most difficult and time-consuming tasks was to get the Home Office to agree that we could produce the licences as continuous stationery so they could be churned out by the computer. We were given many reasons why it was impossible, but it all boiled down to the fact that no-one had ever done it this way before. In spite of the objections, we eventually got the system up and running. Until then, there had been no information available about shotgun ownership, and I was greatly satisfied when as a result of our producing a computer listing of shotgun owners in a particular area, the police were able to arrest a man who had wielded one in an armed robbery of a rural sub-post office.

After this there was the rather less glamorous task of using the computer to produce an internal telephone directory for County Hall. It turned out well, and was pretty unremarkable, except that while we were collecting the information, it became obvious that both the county council and Post Office Telephones had only the haziest idea of the numbers, types and locations of the many telephones in use in the building, and that our phone bills for years must have borne very little relationship to reality.

Next came the registration of electors. The annual production of the electors' register was an intensely time-consuming and costly job, with high print costs. This was a listing process ideal for the computer, and we embarked on the gigantic task of dealing with the county's five parliamentary constituencies one by one.

Like most initial transfers of information from manual to electronic systems, it was monotonous work checking that entries were correct. Leader of the small, dedicated team of checkers was a retired member of the diplomatic service, who livened things up no end with tales of his experiences around the globe. He had started his career in the Indian police, from where he was seconded to help arrest collaborators and other criminals in Indo-China after the Japanese surrender at the end of the war. He then went back to the Indian police until independence was declared, and from there into the diplomatic service.

From his anecdotes we learned of his dealings with President

Tubman of Liberia, where there was some suspicion of oiling the wheels of diplomacy with cases of Black and White Scotch whisky. Another tale from Liberia concerned the uneasy relationship between the traditional medicine and magic administered by witch-doctors and western medical practice, which, it seemed, sometimes required some pretty quick thinking. He told us about a girl visiting a European doctor who, after examination, declared her to be pregnant. She protested heatedly that this wasn't possible because she had been given an anti-pregnancy device by the local witch-doctor. Carefully the European medic asked her the nature of the device, which turned out to be a cord which the witch-doctor had instructed her to wear while making love with her boyfriend. Knowing that making a statement which conflicted with the witch-doctor's wisdom would only cause trouble for himself, the medic enquired where she had worn the cord. "Around my neck," she said. "You are a silly girl," said the doctor. "You were supposed to tie it around your legs above the knees." Thus the honour and reputation of all, except that of the girl, were kept intact. Apparently, the Liberian climate was awful for foreigners, and I remember our ex-diplomatic friend telling of sitting on the hot and steamy veranda of the consular residence and dreaming wistfully of Westminster Bridge in the winter rain and fog. Among his many tales of diplomatic life, was the story of the briefing he received while he was British Consul in Cincinnati instructing him to ensure that supplies of gin were left in strategically situated toilets along the route of a tour being made by the Queen Mother.

The electoral rolls revealed some splendidly outrageous examples of names bestowed upon children by their parents. I particularly remember the beautiful alliteration of one named 'Sylvanus Screech'. Other oddities passed before us, including one street of a small town where families of Crowes, Sparrows, Partridges, Pigeons and Ravens lived. One of the curiosities of data input was the fact that if a name was entered wrongly, it sometimes seemed unwarrantedly difficult to get it corrected. I remember one name, Alan Kelly, who persistently appeared on the draft list as 'Anal Kelly'. I'm not sure we ever managed to get it right.

It was now 1969, and these were stirring times. The anarchy

of the French students had largely died down, the decade was drawing to a hedonistic close, and the first man had set foot on the moon, deposited there by a craft controlled by the most sophisticated and up-to-date computer technology from IBM. Meanwhile, I was repeatedly using another version of their product to try to turn 'Anal' into 'Alan'.

The electoral team were not taking kindly to computerisation, which they devoutly distrusted. I was drafted in as a kind of go-between, sandwiched between the technology and a cynical time-served section head who viewed me with great suspicion. Gradually we got to know each other, and I think that one of the things that helped was my desire to see as much as possible of the election system as a whole. He put in a word with the department's admin chief, John Fox, and I found myself becoming a presiding officer in a polling station in one constituency, followed the next day by helping to administer the count at another at the opposite end of the county.

It is now time to meet the clerk of the council, Henry Gardner, who, like most clerks in those days, was a lawyer. He was a dapper man in late middle age, a perfect gentleman to more junior members of staff, but a cause of disquiet to many senior managers because of his liking for playing 'divide and rule'. Mr Gardner (no-one would have dared to call him Henry except his chief officer colleagues) was said to have an immense liking for gin, which, so rumour had it, he consumed in large quantities. This tended to cause consternation to those managers who picked up the telephone on their desk to hear the command 'Gardner here. Will you come to my office?' The opening of any meeting at any time of day was generally accompanied by a gin, which on no account could be refused. The portions of gin dished out were generous, and I believe that some regular attenders habitually positioned themselves close enough to pot plants to dispose of the drink surreptitiously, and thus maintain a little sobriety. Mr Gardner was not, apparently, totally immune from the effects of gin himself. He once fell up the main steps of the building, reputedly under the influence, and sprained an ankle. Because he was of such status in the organisation, none other than the county nursing officer was summoned to administer a dressing. Although this was the age of the breathalyser, Mr Gardner never had a problem with driving, because he had a car supplied by the Council and chauffeured by a driver possessed of flawless discretion.

The administration of general elections and the announcement of results are always in the hands of a person who bears the temporary title of 'acting returning officer', and one of the privileges enjoyed by the clerk of the council in those days was that he could choose which constituency in his bailiwick would enjoy his presence in that role. Mr Gardner tended to favour the constituency where I was to help with the count.

This was before the time of the present practice of counting the votes immediately after polling stations close. The counting of our constituency's votes took place in a large assembly room in a Victorian gothic town hall the day after voting. John Fox was in charge. Everything went smoothly, except that I seemed to spend quite a lot of time shooing one of the candidates – a Conservative who later spent time as a high-ranking cabinet minister – away from the table where the counted votes were lodged. This was forbidden territory except to those administering the process. We didn't see too much of Mr Gardner for most of the count, the formal process of which was due to finish about midday. I think that the gin had called him into an adjacent hotel.

He appeared, a little worse for wear, towards the end of the process when we were dealing with spoiled ballot papers. A spoiled paper is one on which a voter does not indicate their preference by marking the single 'X' required by the system for parliamentary elections. Some voters choose the ballot to vent their wrath about politicians or the system. On this occasion I can remember "You're all bloody useless", "Send them back to Butlins" and "Come back Henry VIII – all is forgiven". The rule with spoiled papers is that the acting returning officer makes the decision about whether the voter's intention is clear from the spoiled paper. This can be crucial in the case of marginal results.

Mr Gardner peered into the box containing the spoiled papers, pulled out a handful, and made his decisions. He selected a paper from his pile. "That's a good one," he intoned, tossing it over his shoulder. "Another good one," tossing the second over his shoulder. "That's not a good one" was the decision on the third, which was duly tossed over the other shoulder. This performance went on until the box was empty, with us scurrying around behind him to catch the papers as they fell. The job completed, he disappeared, leaving John Fox to administer the remainder of the count.

Everything was done, and the result was ready to be announced from the balcony of the town hall by the acting returning officer. The candidates took up their places, but Mr Gardner was nowhere to be seen. A quick dash around did not reveal his presence, and it was obvious that the candidates on the balcony and the crowd assembled in the courtyard below were getting impatient. John Fox decided to take the law into his own hands. He took centre stage on the balcony, and duly read the declaration "I, the undersigned, being acting returning officer for the constituency of....." and so on. The candidates made their speeches, the crowd below applauded fitfully and dispersed. "I wonder where he got to?" said John Fox. Then, as the crowd disappeared, the solitary dapper figure of Mr Gardner was left standing in the courtyard, clapping slowly, swaying slightly and calling out "Well done, Fox! Well done, Fox!"

Associated with the computer system for the registration of electors was another system for producing rate bills. It was inevitable after my skirmishes with electors' addresses that I should become involved with rates. Then, as now with Council Tax, the bills for the rates were sent out by district councils, and we became the production agents for a number of these, because in those days computers were still very large and very expensive, and beyond the reach of many smaller authorities. The system itself was pretty straightforward, but the fun came after the computing bit.

What we needed was a machine, or a set of machines, which 'burst' the continuous printout from the computer into individual forms, folded each one, inserted it into an envelope and then sealed the flap. I was despatched with a colleague to an office equipment exhibition in London to view the possibilities.

The colleague in question was Ron Vincent, known as Vince, a man steeped in public service who, with the exception of the war years, had worked for local government all his life. He was short, with a twinkling eye, and was full of stories and anecdotes. Vince had grown up in Weston-super-Mare, and had joined the council there in the 1930s. He spoke frequently of his early life, full of amateur dramatics and Methodism (his was a happy sort of Methodism, and he had little time for those he termed 'miserable Methodies') in this seaside resort. He talked about trips on a struggling and run-down minor railway called the Weston, Clevedon & Portishead and reflected on the curiosity of this little local line which was known as the WC & P. From Weston Vince had migrated to a Merseyside authority, where his duties included the collection of council house rents, often carried out by waiting outside men's workplaces on pay-day and extracting cash from them before they were able to get to the pub.

Vince spent the war in the RAF as a navigator in Bomber Command. One of his many stories from this time concerned the homing pigeon which aircraft took on operations to be released with information about the aircraft's position in case of emergency. On one particular type of aircraft there was little room for the navigator, his tools and papers, and the pigeon in a carrying case with its head sticking out. It still seemed to irk him that while he was immersed in navigational duties, the bird had consumed his sandwiches.

Vince had moved from Merseyside after the war, and eventually gravitated into O&M, at which he was a natural. His knowledge of office machinery was second to none, and he had the facility of being able to detect an inefficient or pointless work system from a hundred yards. There was just one problem: he had the uncanny facility of being able to disrupt demonstrations of machinery just by his very presence. He must have emitted some vibrations, unknown to science, which caused mechanical or electrical chaos. It occurred so frequently that it was known as 'Vince's jinx', and he was rather proud of it. It was, therefore, almost inevitable that our trip to London was to leave a wake of frustrated sales representatives and confused engineers. There was one stand at the exhibition which was demonstrating exactly the kind of system that we were looking for. We stood for a time at some distance watching machinery whirring and clunking efficiently, neatly performing all that it was designed to do. Continuous paper forms were churned out by a printer, were burst and trimmed, and beautifully folded and inserted into envelopes, which were then sealed and neatly stacked.

Vince said to me, *sotto voce*, "This could be worth watching", as we stepped on to the stand. A representative, armed with brochures came forward and greeted us warmly. Vince had just started explaining our needs and our potential budget when all hell was let loose. Continuous stationery was suddenly distributed in all directions, the bursting operation became a tearing of paper, and empty envelopes were thrown into the air. The horrified representative and his colleagues rushed around and switched things off, and tried to tidy the chaos, while still trying to engage us as possible customers.

I was sometimes saddened by the way in which the potential of computer systems seemed to be overlooked. For a few months we had a university student attached to the systems team. He was called Taj, came from Tanzania, and we became good friends. His mission while with us was to write a program for something called Critical Path Analysis. This was a technique that had very much taken my fancy during my course in London, where an enthusiastic speaker from the construction industry had introduced us to this method of project planning. Taj bounced a few ideas off me and many of my colleagues from time to time, and eventually wrote what we believed was the first ever viable British local government computer system for using Critical Path, but when it was done, none of the civil engineers, who might have gained great benefit from using it, seemed very interested. Critical Path Analysis was originally developed from a United States Navy system called 'PERT', and perhaps we made a mistake in quoting this pedigree to those who might have benefitted from its use. We knew it was doomed when we heard a very senior person holding forth loudly: "We don't want any of this American stuff round here!"

4

LAYING VIRGINS

The nature of technology and the work changed quite quickly, and I found myself gravitating more and more towards O&M, very often in the company of Vince.

As I became more involved, I wrote more: not just reports, but papers that went to the department's governing committee.

On one occasion, I produced what I thought was a document which covered all the points needed, and which, when typed up, filled about three quarters of a page. I passed it to my manager, who at this time was a person of the Old School. After a few minutes of reading he came over to my desk, where he tutted gently and shook his head.

"I'm afraid this won't do," he said.

"I thought I'd covered all the points," I said, rather taken aback.

"Oh," he replied, "there's no doubt that you've covered everything, but it's just not long enough. It's about *gravitas*, you see. It's got to *look* important, otherwise the elected members won't read it."

This little episode taught me an important principle of local government: if you make something look complicated enough, no-one is likely to query it because no-one wishes to appear ignorant. Thus, you will tend to get what you want.

Bullshit, it seemed, really *did* baffle brains.

Of course, not all local authorities were unfailingly backward, and not everyone who worked for them were mindless operators of inefficient or obsolescent ways of doing things. To be sure, there was a strong dinosaur tendency in some quarters, but there were heroes who, maybe for personal reasons, tried to resist some of the worst aspects of bureaucracy and pointless hard labour. One such was the chief clerk of the Architect's Department.

The authority had acquired a new county architect. His predecessor had been a quiet and gentlemanly person, who greatly encouraged members of his staff who performed well or showed promise (and who had a very nice secretary). He was not, perhaps, the most dynamic of individuals, but he had become well respected during his time with us. The new man was the opposite – dynamic, demanding, autocratic and determined to change things (though the nice secretary remained). Not long after his arrival on the scene, in the cause of change, he summoned the chief clerk. This somewhat wily gentleman, named Geoff Smith, had been around for a while, and knew well how the world of bureaucracy ticked.

The ensuing conversation went something like this:

New Architect: Ah, Smith!

Geoff Smith: Yes, sir?

NA: Would you agree that we have a lot of valuable equipment in the department?

GS: Yes, I suppose we have.

NA: You know, drawing boards, instruments and the like.

GS: Yes, you're right, sir.

NA: I think we ought to identify that we own all the stuff.

GS (having a dreadful inkling about what might be coming): Sorry, sir. I don't think I'm with you.

NA: I mean, we ought to have the council's name engraved or printed on everything.

GS (still playing dumb): Sorry, sir. I'm still not certain what you are suggesting.

NA (losing his rag a little): I'm suggesting that our name ought to be on everything to show ownership.

GS (having had his worst fears of a huge amount of work confirmed, and becoming even dumber): I'm still not absolutely clear.

NA (now truly ratty): Like this, Smith! Like this! (Picking up a ruler upon which was inscribed the name of his previous county council employer, and pointing to it) Like this!

GS (quite gently): And a fat lot of good it did them, didn't it, sir?

Geoff turned on his heel, left the room, and nothing more was heard of the idea.

One day we were asked by the Education Department to help with updating parts of their filing system for property records. At that time anyone who was anyone at the top end of the Education Department seemed to be a devout Christian, usually a nonconformist. I remember taking the brief for the work from an unsmiling assistant education officer, clad, as they all were, in a dark suit, white shirt and sober tie, and noticing during our conversation that the bookcase behind him (obligatory in all top-enders' offices) contained nothing but copies of the Holy Bible. This unsmiling seriousness was the prevailing culture in the department and I was pleased that I had avoided being placed there when I joined the council.

As with everywhere else in the council there were a large number of people who had been on the payroll for a long time and who were not receptive to new ideas, and the new filing system was not easily implemented. A number of visits were made to the quiet and sedate office from which sites and buildings were administered, and some information was grudgingly given, but there always seemed to be good reasons why nothing should change. One man in the office always seemed particularly preoccupied by whatever was on his desk, and seldom looked up when I entered the room or was talking to one of his colleagues. Once in the early afternoon, I visited for some information and he was the only person present. His thumbs were supporting his head, which was tilted towards the documents in front of him, and his fingers shielded his eyes. I stood by him for several minutes, giving the occasional gentle cough, and still he did not look up. He was, in fact, enjoying his habitual post-lunch siesta.

Another Education job concerned an enormous comprehensive school, which had been created by combining two secondary modern schools and one grammar school, on sites which were split by a busy road and whose extremities were about three-quarters of a mile apart. We had been asked to look at the admin arrangements at the school, which was also suffering with the growing pains of the raising of the school leaving age from fifteen to sixteen. There were so many members of staff that they could never meet as a full team, the pupils spent hours each week just moving from site to site and on the surface the place seemed impossible to govern as an entity. Two or three of the teaching staff made comments about the raising of the school leaving age, typified by the observation that "What the kids who are forced to stay on really want is to be mechanics or hairdressers, not another year of sitting in a classroom." It seemed that the lack of motivation was spreading from the pupils to the staff. I never actually wrote any situation off as impossible, but this one came close.

I shared my reservations about the Education Department with Vince, who had seen most things before. He agreed that in many respects that it was a curious mixture of conformism and anarchy, and most bits of it at grassroots level tended to do their own thing. A few years before, he had come across a very small rural primary school in the county where there had been but one member of teaching staff. This man was an obsessive bee-keeper, and his life revolved around bees. So, therefore, did that of the school. In English, the children wrote about bees, in nature study the bee occupied most of their time, in art they drew pictures of bees, and in arithmetic most of the problems revolved around bees, along the lines of "if one bee collects an ounce of pollen in two months, how much pollen will three bees collect in one month?"

By now I was fully inaugurated as a 'travelling officer', and this gave heaven-sent opportunities to get out of the confines of the office and on occasion to join the phalanx that departed from the building before 11.30am on sunny days. The 'sow' had long been replaced, firstly and briefly by a clapped-out Mini, and then by an Austin Healey Sprite, a Mark III, in British Racing Green.

At this time I was suffering from the distress of a broken engagement (remember the nice secretary who worked for the county architect?) and because of that I decided that I would face the world with a new image. I paid a little more attention to my sartorial turnout. The trousers became more flared, the ties more kipper, and, the crowning glory (at least I thought so), was that I was the first in my department to sport a pink shirt. The latter caused some consternation among some of my more staid colleagues, and one older man actually took me aside and said, shaking his head, "I wouldn't wear that when you are representing the Department; it won't go down well." I regret I paid little attention to his exhortation, and continued to demonstrate my new image. It wasn't only at work that this met with disapproval. I visited my elderly grandmother, driving the British Racing Green Sprite and wearing the pink shirt. Grandmother was nothing if not a traditionalist, with a strong streak of the puritan, and I got a good dressing down. "That's not a proper car, and your shirt is awful. Only girls wear pink!"

About this time the county management services officer, otherwise known as Fierce and Remote, got himself another job. He was not the best-loved of individuals, because besides being fierce and remote, he had some habits which did not endear himself to those around him. One of his less attractive attributes came into play when he represented his department at committee meetings. If reports and papers met with approval, and occasionally enthusiasm, he was very happy to take the credit himself, and the happiness and enthusiasm were not passed to the people who'd created the reports in the first place. Conversely, if things were greeted with black looks and disdain from a disagreeing committee, Fierce and Remote was more than happy to endorse the negative comments, and to attribute blame to particular members of staff, who on his return to the department were summoned to his office for a good ticking off.

Perhaps because of this, the customary collection for a farewell present on his departure did not amount to the biggest pot of cash ever seen. Nevertheless, enough for a very reasonable fountain pen was gathered in, and a brief presentation was made on Fierce and Remote's last afternoon by Vince, who was the longest-serving member of the team.

On Vince's return to the office, I asked how the presentation had gone. "OK, I suppose," he said. "The bugger never smiled, but then he never does, and his thanks were very abbreviated." At that moment, the phone on Vince's desk rang. It was Fierce and Remote, demanding that Vince should immediately attend upon him. Vince bustled out of the room, to return furious a couple of minutes later. "The bugger's true to form, right to the last!" he said through gritted teeth. "When I went in, he said snootily 'Vincent, you know better than most that I never use anything other than black ink. This fountain pen has a blue ink cartridge. Go into town straightaway and buy me some black ink cartridges.' And he never even gave me any money to do it with!"

Fierce and Remote was replaced by Benign and Fatherly, a change which was much appreciated. Benign and Fatherly was a man who was so generous to his staff that he was incapable of admonishment. One day, he sent for me – I knew why and presented myself a little nervously. I had transgressed and deserved a good talking-to. The ten-minute chat that ensued skirted all around the matter in question, and instead of leaving the interview feeling chastened, which was certainly what I deserved, I felt almost as though I was going to get a pay rise. Another memorable characteristic of Benign and Fatherly was his ability to misapply or distort the English language. He referred to things called "pet noires" – was this a black poodle or a pet hate? – and once bustled out of his office to go to a meeting telling his secretary that he would be "cascaded" if he was late.

As might be imagined, the business of Organisation and Methods was not loved by the rest of the County's payroll. This was quite understandable, really. If people had been plodding along, sometimes for years, doing jobs whose *raison d'etre* was highly questionable or had ceased to exist altogether, or if they had constructed little empires which were of doubtful benefit to the organisation, it was not unnatural that they would feel hurt or put upon or angry when there was a suggestion that the jobs of dubious value should disposed of, or the empires reduced or disbanded. As an O&M specialist, I was not, therefore, the most popular man at the council.

I remember a local newspaper review of my performance in an amateur dramatics production. The review was seen by the editor of the council's staff magazine. The magazine was published by the local branch of the trades union which, naturally, had a vested interest in preserving jobs, regardless of how useful they were.The editor made sure that an extract from the review was reprinted: "Malcolm Philips gives a highly credible and convincing performance as a Cockney spiv, always wheeling and dealing, the kind of character who would sell his grandmother for the price of her socks." The editor added the slightly tart editorial observation that "Malcolm is a well-known member of the council's O&M team."

One of the growth areas at the time was in another almost lost art: time and motion study, also known as 'work study'. This was the process of observing work being done, and producing standard times for how long each task took to complete. Local authorities started taking notice of it because of a circular from the government of the day which, in a belated, and probably vain, attempt to curb public expenditure, said that pay rises for that breed of people described as 'manual workers' must be linked to increases in productivity. This bred a plethora of bonus schemes, all based on work study, and a consequent demand for staff to become 'work study' experts.

The council already had a small work study team, but they were hard-pressed to cope with demand, so a few of us from O&M were asked to step into the breach as 'stop-watch bashers'. We were issued with clipboards, slide-rules for complex calculations, and stop-watches that counted time in decimal minutes (100 of these to the hour). We were then let loose to observe the goings-on of cynical and uncooperative gangs of workers.

One of the things which didn't seem to be taken into account was that when people are watched at work, and they know that the watching will eventually give rise to a system which will affect their wages, they tend to slow down, and become very methodical and detail-conscious, with scrupulous attention being paid to safe practices and the like. Many years after the events recounted here, I remember challenging our village postman when he arrived to enjoy his Saturday lunchtime pint in the pub.

"What's happening?" I asked. "You were late delivering my post this morning and now you're late for your pint."

He grinned wisely. "Well, you see, I've had this work-study bloke riding in the van this week, so I've been doing everything properly. No hopping over the fences between houses – I've used the front gates every time. And no more dropping off Stan's post at his uncle's house: it all had to go to the address on the front of the letters. So it took a lot longer than usual. Might mean I get more overtime in future, though."

It was nice to find that things hadn't changed much since my time with the stop-watch.

There were exciting jobs to be done in work-study, such as leaping on and off the back of the dustcarts while watching the bin-men at work, but temporary members of the team like me were never given these tasks. Mainly, we were sent to places like school canteens. In most of these, because we were seen to be arbiters of future rewards, we were fed regally and plied with constant cups of tea by the hardworking kitchen staff. We observed not only the preparation of the food, but its serving methods, and the washing-up process. For some of the time during the school canteens exercise, teachers were 'working to rule' and refusing to supervise the dining area. I remember observing the process of serving lunches at a grammar school of reasonable reputation, where the only visible member of staff in the dining room was the headteacher, who frowned upon such industrial action. He sat in glorious isolation at a table of his own, feebly trying to stop, and occasionally having to duck, the sporadic hail of food, particularly roast potatoes, being thrown around by pupils.

More impressive was the performance of the headmistress of the neighbouring secondary modern school, who had run a borstal establishment earlier in her career. The pupils at the school were generally well behaved and smartly turned out, and I was struck with her approach to the beginning of each working day. Instead of walling herself up in her office, or mixing with teaching colleagues in the staffroom, her first action was always to have a meeting with the non-academic team leaders. Thus she met the caretaker, the groundsman, the senior secretary and the cook-supervisor for a two-way briefing session to highlight matters for the day. The head knew that without these people's teams being closely involved, the school could not operate effectively, and the sense of status and belonging imparted to those who attended the meeting was obvious. It was the very reverse of the sometimes often heard mantra from some teachers about 'we professionals'. The message was clearly given that everyone, regardless of their role, was a professional.

I did get to do one or two work-study jobs with road workers. Little could compete for lack of excitement with watching the laying of kerbstones or the cutting of grass verges, but it was quite fun if the weather was good. There were occasional moments of pathos. I remember the foreman of a small gang building a dry-stone wall almost in tears as he protested that it was impossible to put standard times on the act of searching for appropriate stones in a random heap. He viewed the impending bonus scheme as the destruction of traditional crafts, and I must admit that I had some sympathy with him.

Once the bonus schemes had been created, the workers had to complete timesheets detailing the tasks they done and the time taken. Then came numerous calculations based on standard times, carried out by a roomful of people called bonus clerks. There were a few machines, all mechanical, to help with the arithmetic, but it quickly became obvious that something more sophisticated was needed. The council bought four desktop electronic calculators. About a foot square and mains operated, they had no memory and performed only the four basic arithmetical functions. They were state of the art. Only about a year after they were bought, I was talking to an office equipment supplier, who was demonstrating his latest wonder – a battery-operated machine only about six inches by four, with an LCD screen, a memory and percentage function. I remarked how calculators had shrunk and become more sophisticated in merely a year, and wondered what the future would hold. The representative was adamant that things had been developed about as far as they could, and what we were looking at was unlikely to be surpassed.

The team of bonus clerks grew rapidly, and they were housed in a ground floor office with windows that looked out onto a neighbouring street. Most of the recruits were rather plain women, and there was a rumour that the work study officer, who made the appointments, shied away from recruiting attractive ones because his wife, a woman not to be trifled with, regularly walked down the street to look through the windows of the bonus clerks' office to make sure that he was not employing tempting beauties. The bonus clerks had little idea about what many of the tasks described on the timesheets were, and sometimes the way in which the sheets were filled out was not helpful. Words written with a blunt pencil in the rain while using a concrete block as a desk were not always easily translated, and there were sometimes questions over literacy and the use of words. One example which caused great amusement came from a road worker employed in turfing the area between pavement and highway, who claimed that he had spent most of the week "laying virgins".

After my stint at work-study, I retreated once more into the world of O&M.

Like all large bureaucracies, the council had a central purchasing department. The economies of scale ruled. Bulk buying meant bargaining power, and bargaining power meant good price reductions by suppliers. Local purchasing by individual units of the council was taboo. Buying a tin of plasters at the local chemist, for example, was not allowed, because central purchasing could get it at half the price. The mere fact that the person needing the plaster might bleed to death while waiting the two weeks for delivery apparently counted for little.

A prime example of this bulk-buying philosophy was the case of the chefs' hats. Traditionally, all the people who managed school canteens – the cook supervisors – were women, but once upon a time a man was appointed. The women wore traditional kitchen headgear, but someone decreed that the man should be issued with a proper chef's hat, and our friends in the purchasing department got to work and secured an excellent quantity discount for a pile of hats. The new chef was duly issued with a couple of hats, and, for all I know, an extra one for a rainy day, and the rest of the pile was taken into stock, where they remained and remained, being carefully counted at each stock-take for years and years.

I was asked to look at the whole business of how the purchasing department dealt with orders from various parts of the council, because there was a feeling that the service provided was pretty poor. Having gleaned order-handling experience in the world of commerce, I was pleased to have a go at this and to have the chance to employ a bit of creative thinking. I suggested that the purchasing department install a telesales office to take orders, and that all the paperwork should revolve around an order document which was completed manually with a series of bar marks which could be read electronically into the computer, which in turn would churn out delivery notes, and manage stock control and almost everything else. I felt quite proud of my final proposition.

But it failed to tickle the fancy of the established bureaucracy, which hummed and ha'd, and eventually put it quietly aside, with one of the time-honoured statements beloved of those who wish to adopt the easy route and to continue with the status quo: "I see what you mean, but I don't think we're quite ready for this yet".

5

A BRUSH-OFF FROM THE TYPING POOL

In the absence of a more formal approach to personnel management, from time to time O&M people were drafted in to do 'staffing studies', in a forlorn attempt to stop the inexorable growth in the number of people on the council's payroll. Any department wanting to take on more people had to justify it.

I became familiar with a couple of the bits of jargon which underpinned this growth in headcount, one of which was 'the revenue consequences of capital expenditure'. This referred to the fact that in those days, particularly in public service, much trumpeting occurred when a new project – an extra old folks' home perhaps – was planned and built, but sometimes the running costs seemed to be conveniently ignored. Maybe it was a lack of a business sense, or just that fact that for years the public purse had seemed bottomless – more money seemed always forthcoming from the public, either directly or via the government – and some of the people in charge didn't much care. Whatever the project was, it was deemed necessary, and therefore it happened. This in turn, together with changes in working practices or technologies, contributed to another jargon phrase – 'creeping incrementalism' – which described the constant year-after-year increases in budgets.

My first skirmish with staffing studies was also one of my least comfortable. A major department, renowned for the production of many official documents and much correspondence, said that it needed more typists. We had to try to determine whether or not the existing typists were being employed efficiently. I was despatched to the typing pool to observe what was going on and note down the activities that were being carried out. As might be imagined the typists were not exactly happy about this, and when I took up my duties on a Monday morning, I found myself consigned to an uncomfortable chair in an open part of the office. The girls in the typing pool largely ignored me, and there were muttered references to my presence from various visitors delivering and collecting work, such as "new boyfriend?" (snigger, snigger). My occasional efforts at polite conversation were also ignored, and I was pleased when after two or three days I was relieved of my duties. The outcome? We gave in, and approved the extra pairs of hands.

The hotchpotch of departments and sub-divisions of the average local authority had come about because it had grown like Topsy: every time the council had to take on new duties, another department or section was shoehorned in. Every now and then an attempt was made to tidy things up in the hope that they would work better. One such attempt was triggered by the Seebohm Report of 1968, which suggested merging children's services, welfare provision and a few bits of fringe healthcare into a new entity called Social Services. For our authority this meant a splendid upheaval, much talk of structure plans, salary scales and job titles, and the calling in of O&M to try to create a bit of order.

Some of the job titles that were dreamed up sounded very important, but because they were so lengthy they were often abbreviated and referred to by their initials. Thus, those entitled 'senior officer, residential and daycare services' became known as 'SORDS', and so on. A job to be called 'principal officer, finance, training and administration' was also mooted, but never became an entity, maybe because some perceptive person thought about the initial letters, and imagined what, with a little adaptation, the proud job-holders might become known as.

As the dust of reorganisation was settling I was asked to look at the case for an extra admin person in one of the outlying Social Services divisional offices. There were only two admin jobs in the office, improbably entitled 'senior divisional administrative officer' and 'deputy senior divisional administrative officer'. In spite of the grand titles, both posts were paid on lowly clerical grades, but because there was so much more paperwork to deal with than had been envisaged originally, they needed another, even more lowly, person. Sadly, I never found out what it was intended to call the new proposed job, but 'assistant deputy senior divisional administrative officer' ought to have been a contender.

I visited the office, and a pleasant, long-serving, senior social worker told me why the new job was needed: to support the social workers who were out in the field. I felt I needed to grasp a little more about the whole business, because I only had a hazy idea of what social work actually entailed, so I asked him to give me some examples. He didn't pull any punches, and shone the light upon some of the more curious and unpleasant things that social workers had to face, such as reacting to the behaviour of people with serious mental illness, or dealing with the aftermath of child abuse With my sheltered approach to life I was rather taken aback at some of the sharp detail.

"How on earth can anybody undertake this sort of stuff as a profession?" I asked him.

He gave a wry grin: "Well, a lot of social workers have *their* needs, too, you know."

Being a local authority serving a large population, we had a large number of Old People's Homes, as they were then called. These varied widely in terms of size and pedigree. Modern purpose-built places were staffed in the same way as much older buildings which had once served other purposes. This clearly made no sense, and so a couple of us were charged with developing formulae for staffing numbers based upon such fascinating items as floor coverings and room dimensions. We visited every home, talked to staff, matrons and residents, and compiled copious notes on our clipboards.

Once more, as 'men from head office' we were viewed with suspicion, and a number of matrons made it quite clear that they believed that outsiders like us could not possibly have any idea about what went on, or make any valid judgements about staff numbers and duties. They may have had a point. Certainly I can remember one or two going out of their way to ensure that we experienced the full range of aspects of life in the care business, including copious exposure to the effects of incontinence and its resulting ordure and odour.

Some matrons were extraordinary characters who wouldn't have been out of place in films or literature. I remember one large and rambling former hotel in a rather unfashionable seaside resort which was governed by a small, fierce woman who was married to a fisherman and who had two pet whippets which were the apples of her eye. I soon figured out that the toughest fisherman would have quailed before a verbal frontal assault from the lady in question, who ran an extremely tight ship of her own. I was saved only because the whippets took a liking to me, and leapt on my lap the minute I entered her office. This apparently meant that I was 'OK', so our discussion went well.

Fierceness was not off the agenda, however, as I learned when I made a return visit to inform her of the results of our research. The usual fear among those in charge was that we would recommend reductions in staff numbers, and for that reason our approach was always gentle and somewhat circumspect. This was not allowed here: the matron came straight to the point.

"What are you going to tell me, then?"

I smiled winningly. "Well, actually, I've got some rather good news for you."

"What's that?" she said, looking at me stern-faced.

"Our calculations show that you actually need two extra care assistants and one extra member of domestic staff."

She snorted. "Are you telling me that I don't look after this place and the people in it properly?"

"No, no, of course not."

"Don't need them, and don't want them. This is my job, and I don't want anyone telling me how to do it!"

And try as I might, I couldn't get her to accept the extra help. I had a passing thought that maybe a few more like her would be good for local government.

Another place we visited was a gaunt Victorian building converted from a workhouse to a reasonably comfortable residential home, but it retained something of the atmosphere of the original. It was run by a husband and wife team who were not unkind, but still had something of the 'master and mistress' about them. We had the usual meeting in their office to explain things, and although they remained rather formal, they seemed to understand what we were about. Then came lunchtime. We repaired to their living quarters, and were somewhat regally entertained with a meal prepared in the home's kitchen, silver-served by a member of staff on classy china. Perhaps shades of the old workhouse still influenced the way some things were done.

In those days, old people's homes had residents who were relatively young by modern standards – some only in their early sixties – and who were completely *compos mentis*. Notwithstanding this, I found it curious and somewhat sad when one social worker shared with me the fact that when he retired he hoped that he could immediately take up residence in a home on his patch which was his favourite. I thought about the smell of the places and the institutionalisation, and wondered ...

The authority had long pursued a policy of creating large comprehensive schools, but had tended to persist with old ideas about staffing. Bigger schools meant more secretarial people who were at the behest of the head. One excellent head, however, who had more than the usual amount of organisational vision, put forward an idea for having an admin manager to look after non-academic affairs. I was asked to visit the school to learn more of the idea, and it very quickly became obvious that the concept was a good one. The place was well organised, and the notion of an admin manager was spot on. "After all," said the head, "if private schools have bursars, why shouldn't the state sector have them, too?"

The appointment was approved, and the head, with whom I had struck up a good relationship, asked me if I would help write a job description, and be part of the selection interview panel. Although somewhat short of experience in recruitment, I readily agreed.

When the day came for the interviews we had five reasonable-sounding candidates. The interviewing panel was also five strong, and included not only the head and me, and a couple of senior teachers, but also the chairman of the board of governors, an old man well into his seventies who was hard of hearing but in denial about it. This didn't seem to me to be much of a help in listening to the candidates' contributions, but it turned out not to be too much of a problem because he dozed off during the second interview, and was sound asleep shortly afterwards. It was a warm day, and we had the windows wide open. The final candidate finished his contribution, was thanked, and stood up to go. As he left the room a maverick gust of wind came through the windows, and slammed the door noisily behind him. The chairman of the governors woke with a start, jumped forward in his chair, pointed an aguey finger in the direction of the closed door and said "That's the man. He's the best we've seen today."

The county contained a couple of large country parks, and these were patrolled and maintained by a small number of wardens. It seemed that other local authorities tended to be more generous to these sorts of people than we were, and the wardens lobbied their departmental head for a review of their hours and equipment. The review was duly handed to us, and I was given the pleasant task of visiting the two head wardens on their respective native heaths to discuss things with them.

    The first one had the largest area to look after, and was very much the country gentleman. He had a double-barrelled surname, and sported mustard-coloured trousers, brown brogues, a tweed jacket, cravat and a checked cloth cap. The brogues were occasionally exchanged for green wellington boots for work in wet and muddy conditions, when a green waxed jacket was also donned. Very much at home in his environment, he was happy to act as my host for a tour of his domain and to tell me his views about the job. On a gloriously sunny summer's day we rode around in his county-provided Land Rover, lunched at a pub where he knew everyone by name, and had a gentle viewing of a few of his current projects, among which were the clearing of footpaths, and erection of stiles and signposts. The head warden remarked that the signposts had to be checked very carefully because they were produced in the workshop of a local prison, and although the work of the inmates was carefully supervised they were forever trying to introduce alternative, and preferably doubtful, alternative spellings of the names shown. Only the previous week the head warden had intercepted one which would have directed lovers of the outdoor life to a 'Campshite'.

The visit to the second country park was rather different. The head warden here was a little more earthy, and suggested that it might be a good idea for me to provide practical help with a couple of tasks he had on hand. It was again a glorious day when we drove off in his Land Rover to site new signposts in holes he had previously dug, and to repair a gate across a footpath. After we had done these things, he parked the Land Rover and we made our way along another footpath.

"The weather's right and there's something I want to show you," he said mysteriously, as we left the footpath and struck out across a heather covered expanse of open country. We rounded a rocky outcropping well off the beaten track, and came across two beautifully built young women sunbathing completely naked.

"Morning, ladies. It's another lovely day, isn't it?"

"Hello, again, yes it is lovely," one of them replied unconcernedly. "Do you think it will last?"

"Hope so," said the head warden.

We made our way back to the footpath.

"Thought you'd be interested in that," he said. "They've been there every day this week. Interesting perk of the job, don't you think? Country park people in other places may be better equipped and catered for than us, but I don't suppose they get too much of that, especially up north where it's colder."

Other jobs were far less pleasant.

I joined Ben Pease, a short, cynical and amusing man who had studied at the feet of Vince, for a return to academia with a visit to a college of further education which was asking for more admin staff. The two of us spoke with various people and when we compared notes at the end of the day we were both clear that the real problem was not that there weren't enough staff, but that there was a problem with the way the place was managed, the attitude of some of the most senior managers, and the way the work was distributed and carried out.

The problem was that the principal of the college was a despot, and had a completely justified reputation for not only being prickly, but downright difficult, with a strong tendency towards nasty if crossed. Ben and I finally decided that after getting our evidence in order we would ask our chief to come with us for our next meeting with the principal, when we would need to suggest to him that certain changes in their chaotic work systems would need to be made before we could consider any possibility of extra staff.

We put the proposition to Benign and Fatherly.

"What? Are you afraid of him?"

"Of course not," I said. "We're just keen to get a result, and in order to make the principal listen, it would be good to have someone of top status along with us."

"So you *are* afraid of him?"

"Yes, sir."

I think we'd put the wind up Benign and Fatherly, because after agreeing that it would be a good thing, he promptly delegated the task to his deputy, who had no option but to accompany us.

The principal had clearly formed some idea in advance of what was likely to be the thrust of our argument. When we arrived for the meeting, his secretary greeted us icily, and the principal made it quite clear what he thought about us by making us wait while he dealt with ten minutes' worth of trivial matters.

We were eventually summoned, and were seated around a barren table. There was no offer of refreshment.

"Good morning," said the principal. "Well?"

Benign and Fatherly's deputy began to put our thoughts to him. The principal sat grim-faced throughout. After a few minutes which terminated with the thought that we couldn't agree to extra staff until other things had been attended to, the deputy ground to a halt. There was an extended pause, and then the principal took a deep breath and banged his fist on the table.

"How dare you?" he growled. "How dare you tell someone as highly qualified as me how to run his organisation? I know from my qualifications and experience that I need extra staff, and I will get them willy-nilly without stupid people like you getting in my way. Now get out. And I don't want to see any of you on this campus ever again, and that," he said eyeing the deputy and jabbing a finger towards him, "includes you, too."

We beat a retreat, followed by a cold stare from the secretary.

Ben and I were pleased that we had solicited help from the top end of our department, if for no other reason than to provide us with an alibi. The deputy said that he would quickly report events to Benign and Fatherly, which he luckily did just ahead of the arrival of a furious and formal complaint from the principal via the chief education officer the next day. Did we win? No, but at least we got our version of events on the record first.

The council had a department which fascinated me: it dealt with and stored the archives of the county. These were not only council records, but many papers and historical documents from various other organisations and estates.

The county archivist was an incredibly intelligent and knowledgeable man, well known as an eccentric. Some of the eccentricity was allegedly caused by a piece of German shrapnel collected when he inadvisedly stuck his head out of the tank he was commanding during the D-Day landings, and which remained rather close to his brain. Sadly, not everyone could cope with his eccentricity or had much respect for the business of archiving, so when a request was received for some temporary extra help in the building holding the valuable collection, some were loathe to get involved. Because I liked the notion of keeping old records, and because I had never met the archivist, the job came my way.

Followed by the grins and jeers of my colleagues, I left for a meeting with the archivist, and I think I adopted a positive approach to his request. He had thought his proposition through, and explained he needed some help because the archive had recently been bequeathed a large quantity of material from one or two ancient 'manorial domains'. Detecting some interest on my part, he insisted on showing me some of the items. He took me to a shelf full of parchments from the bequests.

"This stuff is about eight hundred years old," he said. He selected a sample that was somewhat screwed up, and under my astounded gaze, he tugged and pulled at the edges to straighten it.

"Tough stuff, parchment," he observed, and then began to read from it. I could scarcely see any writing on the parchment, but he apparently had no trouble, giving me an instant translation from Norman French into modern English.

I recommended some temporary extra help, which was allowed, and received a pleased telephone call from the archivist thanking us. This was a nice thing to happen, but the silver lining dwindled somewhat when it became obvious that from then on I was considered to be the answer to any problem that the Archives Department had. Eventually I had to enlist the help of colleagues to stem the flow of requests.

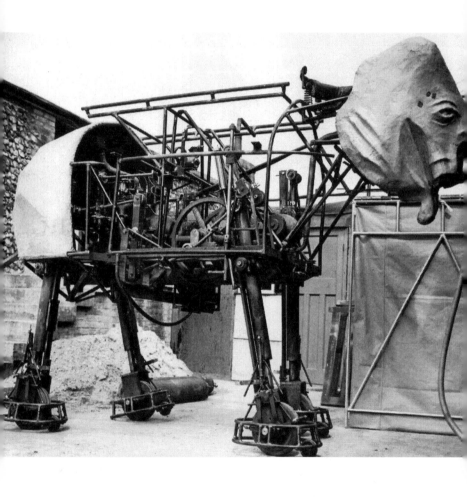

6

REPAIRING THE ELEPHANT

During the 1950s and 1960s there was much discussion about local government efficiency and structure, which ultimately led to its major reorganisation in 1974, but even before this there were locally agreed mergers and revisions. One of these occurred within the boundary of the county council I worked for, and illustrated very well how what was probably acceptable in the nineteenth century didn't always work too well in the twentieth.

A very rural tongue of land protruded from our county into the next. It was sparsely populated and contained no settlements of any size. Nevertheless, the area was governed by its own Rural District Council, which employed three people.

A merger was arranged with the much larger neighbouring Rural District Council, and by all accounts this went very smoothly – indeed, almost unnoticeably. But there was one fly-in-the-ointment connected with the collection of the rents from around 20 council houses. With such a small number of council houses, it was not worth employing a rent collector, and for years this task had been farmed out to a local travelling greengrocer who hawked his produce around the district using a horse and cart. After the merger, it was clearly more sensible to for the collectors from the bigger District Council to do the whole job. Herein lay the rub. It was felt that prising the task away from the itinerant greengrocer was going to be difficult and likely to require much diplomacy, and so it was decided that the head of finance, accompanied by a very junior member of staff, should meet with him face-to-face.

The pair set off in the head of finance's small Austin saloon, and eventually found the greengrocer. A bit of small talk and some beating about the bush ensued, and then the boss bit the bullet.

"It's about the rent collection," he said. "I'm afraid that the Council wishes to dispense with your services."

The greengrocer sucked his breath in, looked glum and shook his head slowly. He said nothing.

"The Council is very grateful to you for all your work over the years, and fully appreciates the problems that this decision might cause you. We are, therefore, willing to pay an appropriate sum in compensation." Both he and the very junior member of staff held their breath, and waited for a financial bombshell.

The greengrocer said nothing for a moment or two, and gazed into the middle distance. He sucked his breath in again and frowned. "There's no denying that it'll make a difference to me," he said.

"How much do you want?"

"It *will* make life difficult," he said. "I'm going to have to ask you for £5."

The head of finance, who administered a budget which was well into six figures, could hardly believe his luck. They bade the greengrocer a rapid farewell, climbed into the Austin and drove back to the office before he could change his mind.

Increasingly, many of the smaller authorities began looking at the way they worked, and sometimes called upon the services of their larger neighbour, the County Council, – in our case this often involved O&M.

My first direct involvement with one of the smaller councils was a visit to a small town – an ancient borough. I was to meet the clerk, a part-time employee, as like many small authorities, the town didn't have enough work to justify a full-time clerk, so used the services of a senior member of a local law firm.

When ushered into the clerk's presence, I was struck by a curious and rather unpleasant smell in his office. I decided not to say anything, and sat down, across from the clerk's large, ancient, leather-covered desk. Strange noises regularly emanated from the desk, making it hard for me to concentrate on the matters in hand. Surely the clerk couldn't be farting? Towards the end of our discussion there was a particularly noisome eruption, and for the first time the clerk felt the need to refer to it.

"That's enough of that!" he said, bending down to reach under the desk. It was then that I saw his large, elderly dog. The clerk looked up again. "Sorry about that," he said. "He's always like this. Hope you didn't think it was me!"

One of the next jobs was for an urban council in the north of the county. They were looking at the cost of wages and enlisted our help for a major job evaluation exercise. Three of us were to undertake the work: me, Ben Pease, and Jim Lane, a dapper ex-serviceman aged about forty.

Jim was an interesting character. The habit of personal smartness had been ingrained in him during his service career, and was always neatly turned out. He was a man of extremely fixed habits. His arrival at work was always to the minute, and he then observed a strict routine. Always in this order, he would take off his suit jacket, brush it with a clothes brush produced from the second drawer down in his desk, insert a coat hanger (inscribed with his name, of course), and hang it on the coat stand in the office. He would then take an apple from his briefcase, and put it in the top drawer of the desk, before revisiting the second drawer to take out a neatly folded yellow duster which was used to reinforce the shine on each shoe. Next he would go to the sash window and lower it by exactly ten inches, and then if it was winter, turn the radiator off, regardless of how cold it might be outside.

As soon as the first of his colleagues arrived in the office, he would intone in a sepulchral voice "Well, here we are at the start of another day of unremitting toil in the service of the ungrateful ratepayer."

Jim's interfering with the window and the radiator annoyed other inhabitants of the office, but since he was always first in, it was something of a *fait accompli*. No-one ever spoke up, but some odd wordless practices developed to cope with the situation. The moment Jim left the office, there would be a rush to shut out the fresh air and reinstate the heat. Upon re-entry Jim would wait until his colleagues were otherwise occupied, and quietly reopen the window and readjust the radiator. The latter was generally accomplished by his leaning against the radiator and surreptitiously adjusting the stop-cock with hands behind his back while having a conversation with the nearest person. This pantomime might be repeated several times during the course of a day.

Jim was a bachelor, although he had a long-term relationship with a senior secretary, somewhat older than himself, from elsewhere in County Hall. The relationship appeared to be fairly passionless, and seemed to revolve around a weekly game of tennis.

Jim made a preliminary visit to the borough which was to be our target, toured the offices, and explained to staff there what was going to happen. He returned with a list of those we were to interview about their jobs, and said that he would prepare a schedule.

This job was a long distance from our base, but because we were working as a trio, and at that time I was running the Austin Healey Sprite, which, of course, had only two seats, I became a passenger in either Ben's tank-like and elderly Standard Vanguard estate or Jim's well-polished Triumph Herald. Ben's estate was an integral part of his annual holiday. Fairly unusually for those days, Ben used all his annual leave in one lump to go camping with his family in the south of France, and for this the big estate was filled completely with all the gear and supplies required for a month. He always reappeared after the break suntanned and relaxed, regaling us with tales of wine consumption, games of *boules* and hair-raising driving. The latter were particularly graphic because this was still the era in France of universal giving-way to any traffic from the right, and I gathered there were many near-misses with tractors emerging from field gates on to major highways at low speeds and assuming the right of way.

Both Ben and Jim had their own philosophies about saving petrol. Ben would cut corners, explaining just how much petrol he could save by cutting all the corners in a longish trip. The estate was clearly a thirsty beast. Jim's approach to fuel economy involved what amounted to cruelty to dumb machinery. He would get into top gear at absurdly low speeds, and would stay in there when slowing down until the engine was juddering and complaining. He would tell anyone who queried his methods that top gear always used less petrol, so the longer it was used, the greater the savings. If Ben's economy was because of the high petrol consumption of his Vanguard, Jim's parsimony was based on an innate desire to look after the pennies.

We showed up at the borough offices and introduced ourselves to the clerk, a laid-back barrister who had done what he described as Important Things in East Africa, was inordinately proud of his Mercedes car, and who loved the wigs and paraphernalia of the law. "You'll find the staff will be very co-operative, gentlemen," he said. Then with a wink he added "Don't go upsetting any of my young women, though, will you?"

Ben, happily married, looked young in his middle age (his wife referred to him as 'Bloody Peter Pan') and still had a bit of an eye for the ladies. I was completely footloose and fancy-free. Neither of us, however, was able to get anywhere near any of the clerk's 'young women', let alone upset any of them. Jim's schedule had made sure that Ben and I were assigned to interview all the male staff and the older women, while he got all the desirable girls for himself. This cast a new light on Jim whose interest in women we had thought to be confined to the tennis-playing senior secretary. We suddenly glimpsed the possibility of hitherto hidden depths.

It came as no great surprise to us, therefore, when it later emerged that he had been having a secret, long-standing relationship with a young female colleague, as a result of which a baby was on the way. The couple left the council as rapidly as they could, and we all kept out of the way of the abandoned and angry senior secretary, who seemed to believe that we were all responsible. A few of us wondered how his new partner would take to a cold and draughty winter regime with an apple a day and every coat hanger identified.

It just so happened that our chief, Benign and Fatherly, had a relative who was a councillor for an Urban District Council governing a decaying seaside town at an extreme edge of the county. It had become obvious to her that all was not well in the council: it all came to a head when the district surveyor was unable to locate the position of some drains which needed repairing. The town's drainage maps had been missing for some years, and when work on the drains was required the usual practice was to dig a trench across the road until the drain was discovered. This time, however, the errant drain had eluded all searches.

Benign and Fatherly was approached by the chairman of the council in question and four of us were chosen to provide help and advice. I was delighted to be paired with Vince, and we set off on a bitterly cold February morning to do our best. It was understood that the job would occupy a number of days, and we could stay overnight in the town, because it would be cheaper and would provide a better use of time than if we commuted each day.

It soon became clear that the loss of the drainage plans was only the tip of the iceberg, and that rather a lot of other things were functioning less than effectively as well.

While Vince talked with the clerk of the Council, I visited the denizens who inhabited what was called the General Office to see how things were going there. Actually, there were only two denizens, a senior and a junior clerk. The senior clerk was inevitably suspicious to start with, so I worked hard to reassure him and eventually we got things on to a conversational level. While we indulged in a mug of tea, the senior clerk remarked that we had come a long way for the visit, and that it must have taken a long time.

"Yes," I replied, "but to save time and money we're staying over."

"Whereabouts?"

I gave him the name of the hotel.

"Oh, they're still open, then?" he said, with apparent surprise.

The visit lost a little of its glamour. But since we seemed to be getting along pretty well, and, thinking about possible delights yet to come, I thought I'd risk another question.

"What is there to do in the town of an evening?"

He thought for a while. "Dunno, really," he said. "I generally goes home and watches television."

The prospect of a bleak evening stretched before me.

The senior clerk then started speaking about his work. One of his major daily jobs was the 'post-in' book. Now I had developed a view about post-in books, which Vince with his great experience endorsed, namely, that they were a waste of time and space, and served no useful purpose whatsoever. For the uninitiated, a post-in book is used to record details of every item of mail received, with the date received, the name of the sender, a summary of the content, and a note of the person to whom it was passed.

The senior clerk's book was a splendid specimen – large, thick and leather-bound, full of neatly written information. I gently challenged its reason to exist, and was informed witheringly that it was probably one of the most important things that the Council had. It took on an average morning about two and a half hours to enter the post and I gathered it was a favourite task that was never delegated, except in times of sickness or leave.

Feigning innocence, I asked the senior clerk to take me through the whole process, and, being treated like a child of substandard intellect, I was taken stage by stage through its completion, and the subsequent passing of the mail to the person for whom it was intended. I felt it was now time to pounce.

"I understand all you have told me, but I'm still not sure that I see the point of the exercise."

The senior clerk sighed. "The point of the exercise is that if anyone ever queries whether the letter was received, we know that it was and when, and who it was passed to."

I indicated the final entry for each item, in the 'To Whom Passed' column. "Let me suppose that I am the district treasurer, and you tell me that you passed a certain letter to me a week ago. Suppose I tell you that I have never seen it. What happens then?"

"Well, you must have done."

"But how do you know?" I remonstrated.

He stabbed the page with his finger. "You must have seen it, because it's in my book here!" he replied triumphantly, obviously feeling that he was administering the *coup de grace* in the argument.

Further discussion yielded no different result, but I was determined to try to prove my point. "Look. When I leave here at the end of tomorrow afternoon, suppose I put the book in my briefcase, and took it away with me, and you never saw it again. What would happen? What would be the result?"

"Wouldn't matter a bit. I've got a new one in the stationery cupboard."

The afternoon saw us transfer our attention to the Treasurer's Department. More evidence emerged that things were not as they should be. The accounts were miles behind, and part of the reason was that the council, having no computer of its own, had hired an unreliable agency in Hertfordshire to carry out the number-crunching for them. Cheques were written by hand after invoices from suppliers had been certified as correct by the people who had ordered the goods or services. Certification was done by writing codes on small slips of paper, which reminded me of my old job in the County Health Department. A major difference, though, was that in the Urban District Council the slips were pinned to the invoices, not stuck to them. The reason for this was that when the cheques had been written, the slips had to be detached from the invoices, sorted and sent to the computer agency.

The sorting process was the work of a junior member of staff, and there was no table in the council offices large enough to accommodate the numerous heaps of slips. So she used the floor. The problem was that the young woman in question was a fresh-air fiend, and even in the cold depths of February when we visited, she would open the window wide, and then get on hands and knees to start creating the piles of paper. Every time anyone opened the door to enter the room, the draught would destroy the piles, and it was touching to see her trying to protect her work from the ravages of nature by using her hands and feet as paperweights.

As we dug deeper into the way the finances were handled we came across other oddities, such as the fact that the council had twenty-six bank accounts, allegedly so that each activity could be controlled properly. There was one for the crazy golf in the park, one for the municipal tennis courts, one for pest control, one for the burial ground, and so on.

Mention of the burial ground allows me to take a slight detour through another curiosity. Some time previously space had run out in the town's municipal cemetery, and a councillor, who was a farmer by trade, generously offered to sell to the council, at a favourable price, part of one of his fields which bordered the town. The council was duly grateful. Unfortunately, no-one remembered that the field was in a particularly rocky area, where the soil was only about a foot deep in some places. This presented a problem when it came to digging graves, and the decision was made to buy the grave-digger a compressor and pneumatic drill. It was a unique state of affairs – certainly I never came across another local authority which had to resort to this kind of machinery to dig holes. So much for bargains.

Back in the Treasurer's Department we looked at the day book, where all income and expenditure was entered. Most of the entries were, of course, run-of-the-mill, but I remember one, repeated regularly, which intrigued us greatly. Frequently, particularly in the summer, the entry 'Repairs to elephant' appeared. In the end, we felt we had to ask, and were rewarded with the information that some years before our visit the Council had purchased from Southport or some resort like it, a mechanical elephant, powered by a Ford V-8 engine, and used to give rides to holidaymakers. After its long service at Southport or wherever, it was pretty well clapped-out mechanically and its new owners were constantly paying out to keep the beast roadworthy. Come to think of it, like every other function, the elephant probably also had a bank account of its own.

After a full first day, Vince and I repaired to our hotel. It was not palatial, and aside from the odd sales rep or two, we were the only residents. Stepping into my room was like stepping into a deep freeze. I searched in vain for a stop-cock to turn the radiator on, and then discovered an electric heater, which came on when a two-shilling piece was put into a slot. Two shillings seemed to last about twenty minutes, and I got through quite a number that night. In the restaurant, Vince and I were the only diners.

What to do for the rest of the evening was the question, and Vince and I mulled over the few alternatives. We were just about to consign the notion of going out somewhere to the scrapheap, because of the freezing cold and the fact that there didn't, as intimated by the senior clerk earlier in the day, seem much to do, when in a room next to the restaurant the local operatic society started warming up to rehearse. However unattractive it had seemed as an option, going out now became a necessity.

We wandered around dead and dim winter streets, and suddenly discovered a cinema. This would pass an hour or two in relative comfort, we thought, as we paid for our tickets to see an inferior spaghetti western paired with some science fiction travesty, which seemed from the lobby cards to have used a few superannuated sets from *2001 – A Space Odyssey*. Our thoughts of relative comfort evaporated when we set foot in the auditorium, which was inhabited by about another dozen hardy cinemagoers. It was as cold as the hotel bedroom, and the Spartan environment was not helped by the fact that all but about the rearmost ten rows of seats had been removed for winter refurbishing. We turned up our collars and hunched in our seats. The copies of the films were so old and scratched that most scenes looked as though they had been shot in the rain, but we stayed for every last minute.

When we talked about the evening on our way back to the hotel it became clear that we both thought the films were rubbish, the admission fee excessive and the comfort (like the temperature) close to zero. But we'd paid our money, and had been determined to last the course come hell or high water.

The Post-In Book King passed me in the corridor the following morning and enquired "Good night, last night?" I grimaced and shrugged. "I did warn you," he grunted, with some satisfaction.

One of the curiosities about this council was the fact that all the elected councillors sat on all the council's committees.

This meant, for example, that they could meet at 6.30pm as the Finance and General Purposes Committee, make some decisions, change seats and titles at 7.30pm, reconvene as the full council, and promptly reverse the decisions previously made in Committee. Don't think that this was simply a possibility. It actually happened.

Eventually the time came for us to present our report.

We attended at a meeting of the full council (although, of course, it also might have been any of the committees). The council chamber was a long narrow room with a long narrow leather-covered table, along each side of which sat the councillors, each with their copy of our report. There was scarcely an air of expectancy, but one or two looked reasonably interested.

We'd never had much to do with the councillors prior to this meeting, but there was one character whose reputation had gone before him. He was an American who, having visited the county as a GI during the war prior to D-Day, and liking the place, had returned to become a naturalised resident after, so the story had it, a post-war spell as a cop in an American police force. He ran a gift shop and a pub in the town, and was seen as a successful businessman. We had been warned that he had a reputation for plain speaking, and he eyed us beadily as we started the presentation of our findings.

As we progressed with our arguments about bank accounts, computer agencies, unnecessary clerical work, and, for all I remember, the elephant, it became obvious that he was not happy with all we were suggesting.

At one point it all became too much for him. He reached into a carrier bag which was on the floor by his chair and produced a clockwork duck, which he duly wound up and placed upon the table, where it waddled among the councillors' papers quacking as it went.

"Gentlemen!" he said. "That duck is talking more sense than you are!"

We were asked to look at another Urban District Council at the other end of the county, which was a totally different experience. The clerk of the council was a jovial man, and most members of the staff were rather pleasant. After our introductory meeting we were of the view that relationships around the place seemed generally good, and not too much seemed to need attention.

The district surveyor, however, was a rather prickly character who, judging by the number of certificates adorning all the walls of his office, must have been one of the best qualified people I have ever met. Not only was there affirmation of his membership of the Royal Institute of Chartered Surveyors and one or two other august organisations, but there were also a number from some more obscure bodies including the Association of Civil Engineers of County Cork.

He had a small team, which included a middle-aged man who seemed incredibly good at organisation and who had immense knowledge, but who was paid on the lowliest clerical grade. I couldn't square his salary with the complexity and scope of his work, and eventually I queried this with his boss, making it clear that one of our recommendations would be that he should receive an upgrade. The surveyor cleared his throat and looked out of the window.

"He used to be on a higher grade," he said.

"What happened?"

"It's a bit of a story," said the surveyor. "In your chats with him you have probably gathered that one of his duties is the organisation of the refuse collection."

I had. The council owned one dustcart, worked by a gang of three men.

"Well, the other year he struck up a relationship with the wife of one of the gang, and because he organised the rounds, he knew more or less exactly where the gang was going to be at any one time, and therefore when the coast would be clear for a visit to her. One day, though, the dustcart broke down, was towed back to the depot, and the chaps finished early. The men went home, and our friend was discovered *in flagrante delicto*. The husband was not happy, and we felt that we had no option but to discipline our friend. Morals aside, he was, after all, doing it in the council's time.

"We weren't sure what to do for the best, so after thinking about firing him, we decided to downgrade him. So if you people recommend an upgrading you're going to open old sores, and make life a bit difficult."

We let sleeping dogs lie.

Another assignment was with a very small urban district council which served a town with a population of about 4,000. The clerk here was a daunting woman, well past retiring age, who occupied the job on a part-time basis. Her husband was also a part-time clerk for another small council elsewhere in the county – probably a unique state of affairs.

The ground floor of the council building was largely occupied by a cashier's office, where rates and rents were paid in. On the day we called in, it had been a tolerably busy morning and the drawer in which the takings were placed was almost overflowing. At lunchtime, the chap manning the counter told his colleague he was taking a break and shut the drawer, leaving a fan of overflowing banknotes hanging out. He went out, the door to the office was left unlocked, and the notes were very visible. This may say something about the honesty of the little town, but it probably says more about the culture of the times, when in small communities of this kind security matters were seldom thought about. What tickled us, though, was the fact that the most prominent piece of furniture in the office was a massive – and I mean massive – safe, which to us as outsiders seemed a reasonably logical place in which to leave the money.

We thought that it might be rather fun to inspect the contents of the safe, and the right moment came when the money was being sorted for banking early in the afternoon. We asked naively if the cash was going to be put in the safe.

"Oh, no," said the rent-collector, "we bank every day."

"Such a waste of a splendid safe."

"Oh, it's most important and we do use it. Do you want to have a look inside?" He produced a bunch of keys which would have done credit to the Bank of England.

The safe was gravely unlocked, the wheel on the front turned and the heavy door opened to reveal a huge space, filled with nothing save a sheet or two of postage stamps.

"Can't leave the stamps lying around. People might be tempted to nick one or two of them," he said seriously.

Adjoining this particular council was another urban district serving an equally small community. With these pair of bedfellows we came across an interesting example of how civic pride sometimes got, and probably still gets, in the way of the effective running of things.

The council we were looking at had a rather splendid dustcart. Admittedly it was secondhand, but it was freshly painted in the council's livery, and positively gleamed. The vehicle was only needed for a few days a week, but in spite of relatively small loads, the council had nowhere to tip the refuse it collected. The reverse of this situation applied in the neighbouring council which was equally small, but had no dustcart. It did, however, possess an extremely spacious and well-situated tip.

Innocently, we wondered why the two neighbours didn't pool resources, but when we suggested this we were met with looks of horror. Our host council evidently felt that their waste was of superior quality to that of the neighbouring council, who I believe held a similar view about the materials put on their tip. The result of this was that, rather than cooperate, both councils used the services of a nearby large rural district council. This meant the dustcart had to make a 25-mile round trip at the end of each day in order to dump its waste. Doubtless en route it passed the dustcart that had been hired by our host's neighbours to collect their refuse.

The hero of the council was a middle-aged woman who had started out in life as a typist, but who had gradually become the clerk's personal assistant, the surveyor's personal assistant, and the general hub of the council's business. She also acted as committee clerk, minuting all the meetings and producing agendas and reports, and was the general administrator of all the council's activities. In spite of this range of responsibilities her pay grade could be described as modest at best, and amazingly the chief tool of her trade was an ancient 'sit up and beg' manual typewriter, a machine completely unsuited to the production of her work.

When we produced our report one of our recommendations was that if her pay couldn't be upgraded, that at least she could be given an electric typewriter. We suggested an IBM machine, which we could have obtained for about £370. Looking over the draft of the report, the daunting part-time clerk peered over her spectacles when she reached the suggestion about the typewriter, and said "I can't disagree with you, but I don't think that the councillors will like it. You must realise that such a purchase would mean a penny on the rates."

Thus it was with many of these small authorities, who were finding it more and more difficult to carry out their statutory functions in straitened circumstances. Another illustration of this penury came from an environmental health officer who had worked for a small urban district council somewhere in the Welsh Marches, where among other things, he was responsible for the council's refuse tip. Not long after he started, newly qualified and full of enthusiasm, he reported to his chief that the tip was a health hazard not only because of the decomposing rubbish, but because it was overrun by rats. He was told curtly that there was no likelihood of any money to pay for the extermination of the rodents, and that if he thought it that important he must devise his own strategy to get rid of them. This he did, buying several gallons of petrol from the local garage. After the petrol was liberally distributed over a small part of the tip he set it on fire. The resulting conflagration spread quite quickly, soon becoming a funeral pyre for the rats and blackening the sky overhead for days. Thus one kind of health hazard was replaced by another.

One of the councils we looked at in our county was one which was rather better off, and which governed two or three up-market, fashionable seaports much beloved of the yachting fraternity. I visited the area to talk to the harbour-master. I had with me a trainee who had been attached to our unit, fresh from university and perhaps a little naive about the ways of the world.

The day was beautifully sunny, and we were deep in a chinwag with the harbour-master on the veranda of his shore-side office when he suddenly excused himself, leapt off his chair, picked up an electric megaphone and shouted in the direction of an incoming yacht "*Grande balise rouge!*"

The newly arrived boat duly attached itself to a prominent red buoy, and the harbour-master returned to continue our chat. The trainee looked at him with admiration.

"Gosh, that was very impressive. How did you know the boat was French?"

"It was flying the French flag," said the harbour-master, dryly.

Councils were not the only organisations we got caught up with. We attended upon one or two other types of public sector provider too, including a couple of local water boards. One of these had a large underground reservoir on land leased from a local farmer. During long summers this reservoir frequently dried up, but luckily the farmer had a couple of boreholes close by which had never dried up in living memory, and so the water board would gladly pump supplies from these and pay him for the privilege. This apparently went on for several years. It was only when some routine maintenance was carried out on the reservoir during a dry period that some large cracks in its walls were discovered. It then became clear that when the surrounding soil dried out, water seeped away from the reservoir into the farmer's boreholes. So not only was he getting rent from the water board for the land occupied by the reservoir, but from time to time he was selling their water back to them.

There is no denying the characterful nature of many of those long gone, really local, local authorities, and the people who made them work, or not, as the case may be. When they drifted into history in 1974, even though most had only existed since the 1890's, some little part of the British fabric drifted away with them. That they were not always up to the job as the years progressed cannot be denied, but in these days of sometimes boring conformity and unsmiling political correctness one cannot but look back with some measure of affection to the uniqueness and curious ways of the old system. This might even apply to those who became elected councillors. There were many characters, some unsung heroes, and some who were perfectly awful. At this distance most seem rather more colourful than some of the worthy and earnest elected members of today. I can remember one urban district council where there was such a strong difference of opinion between a few councillors over some matter that a mass punch-up occurred in the council chamber. And where, now, is the like of the clockwork duck wielder?

7

DO YOU SERVE JEWS?

I don't quite remember how I got caught for it, but I was drafted into being an occasional guide for visitors to County Hall. Quite why many of them came is a bit of a mystery, because it was scarcely a venue brimful of excitement. Some were students from the local colleges and schools, some were young Europeans from language schools or making exchange visits, and some from further afield were directed to us by the Foreign and Commonwealth Office or the British Council.

The usual route for the sightseeing started with a visit to the council's committee rooms (quite grand, high ceilings, leather chairs, marble corridor), and then moved on to the council chamber (very grand, lots of oak, serried ranks of leather chairs and desks in tiers, microphones, coats of arms) where I gave some general chat about the history of local government, what it did, how much it cost and a few other statistics. The next port of call was the reprographics room, where most of the council's printing and copying was done (a bit of action here, with machines churning out stuff and the smell of ammonia from the device used to copy architects' plans and the like). The final stop was usually the computer room (nothing to see except humming metal and plastic boxes with 'IBM' on the front, a sterile atmosphere and a fairly sterile brief talk from the chief programmer). Occasionally we would show small school groups the Education Department's film library, but this was scarcely a laugh a minute, either. Sometimes I took groups to look at our terribly modern telephone exchange (not much action here except "Good afternoon, County Hall" and "Hold the line, I'm putting you through") and, with something of an ulterior motive, groups of trainee secretaries from the local college of further education were shown one of the better-equipped typing pools and introduced to the operators of the golf-ball typewriters or typesetting machines, which were then considered the height of sophistication.

Most of the school and college visits were murderous, with the noisy younger end of market not having the foggiest idea what local government was, and the older batches of the great spotty unwashed (as the late Alan Coren referred to teenagers) who didn't want to be there, anyway. We tended to get the older children at the end of the summer term when the GCE exams had been sat and the school was thrashing around desperately trying to find something to pass the time until the end of term.

Even worse were the visits that I sometimes made to schools to speak about local government. The audiences were usually drawn from fifth and sixth forms, and, again, they didn't want to be there. There are fewer less exciting uses of time than addressing hordes of unwilling adolescents imprisoned on hot sunny afternoons in the cavernous and stark surroundings of school halls. What usually happened was that I was introduced by a member of the teaching staff, who more often than not made some comment about the topic being "really interesting", and who then left rapidly to join their mates in the staffroom for tea or coffee. I did what I could, laboured through the script, and released my prisoners as quickly as seemed acceptably possible.

An exception to these visits was a local private school for girls. These more up-market pupils were also informed in the introduction that the subject was going to be "really interesting", but even though they still didn't want to be there, they were at least more polite about it than those from the state schools. An added bonus was that after these events, I was always invited to the headmistress' study, where she asked solicitously how her 'gells' had been, and hoped that they were courteous and that they had listened. After reassurance on these matters, she was profuse in her thanks, and said: "As a thank you, perhaps you would like a gin and tonic." The bottle of gin, the tonic and a glass were duly produced from a cupboard. With no refrigerator in sight the gin was warm, and the tonic (in a half-empty large bottle) was usually flat.

We did try to do "really interesting" occasionally. From time to time we had visits from gangs of more mature people who were retraining under some government-sponsored scheme, and these were more rewarding because they knew that they would all be looking for work at the end of their course. We worked hard with them to give the impression that the place *was* really exciting and that the kinds of things that we did *were* astoundingly engaging. Over the years we recruited quite a number of useful members of staff from these groups, and when this happened, perhaps curiously one or two of them *did* apparently find their work interesting.

The parties of people from abroad were much more fun.

Exchange or language school students were generally polite, and at least feigned some kind of interest. They were always keen to try out their English, and sometimes insisted on taking a group photograph, with their guide in the centre. They tended to write thank-you letters.

We didn't have many too many visits from adult Europeans in those days, although we did once entertain a

couple of taciturn, dark-suited men from somewhere in the Eastern Bloc. We had been warned in advance by their British 'minder' not to ask too many questions about their homeland or the way it did things. We did, however, receive courteous, if unsmiling, thanks from them at the end of their tour, when they ceremonially presented us with red enamel hammer-and-sickle lapel pins.

The Commonwealth visitors were always enjoyable. Many of them stayed overnight nearby and paid sociable visits to the staff club on the County Hall campus. A number of them were high-ranking public servants in their own lands, and were keen to learn as much as possible about how our county council worked. I remember that those from African countries saw the point of providing education services and things like highways and bridges, but were baffled by the need for social services. This, of course, was a reflection of their own social structures where the extended family or town or village community tended to provide care and support for those in need.

One group largely consisted of people from the Pacific Rim and the Pacific Islands: they were very good humoured and fun to deal with. Two Fijians, who laughed a lot, seriously invited me to their archipelago.

From time to time, our team played host to individual visitors. A man from Somalia was attached to our department for a few days, during which he gave me a completely new understanding of the difficulties of administration in parts of the third world. When I asked him what the Somalian government's biggest problem was in providing services was, he gave me a searching glance and a single word reply – "Nomads". This challenged my naivety, and I suddenly realised how different was a world in which there was no easy tax collection and no comfortable provision of the things that we had taken for granted for years in the UK.

An earnest young German public servant joined us for a while, and a rather nice man he seemed to be. But he did cause a slightly tense moment when, early in his stay, he visited the staff club with us.

"Do they serve Jews?" he asked.

We fumbled for what to say, looking down at our shoes and hoping that someone else would answer. Blessed relief arrived when he clarified his desire: "I would like an orange juice".

PENGUIN BOOKS

LADY CHATTERLEY'S LOVER

D. H. LAWRENCE

COMPLETE AND 3/6 UNEXPURGATED

8

THE MUCKY BOOKS CABINET

Local government 'professionalism' should always have been about doing things brilliantly, but frequently it became distilled into a kind of 'we know best' culture, which meant that people were not listened to and were told what they were going to have, willy-nilly. For the record, it seems to me that nothing much has changed. I first glimpsed the approach in my early days in the county council when I asked a senior officer how he went about making decisions as to where health centres should be opened and what services they should provide. "Well," he said, "we make a professional assessment, tell the committee what is needed, and then we carry on and do it."

In my day, no-one in local government referred to the people who used their services as 'customers'. Social services had 'clients', libraries had 'borrowers' or 'readers', education had 'pupils' or 'students' or 'parents', trading standards had 'consumers', and so on. Customers were what nasty, profiteering, industrial and commercial companies had. What the private sector got up to was treated with more than a sniff of suspicion and much later, when 'customer care' became something of a buzz-phrase, it was an uphill struggle to get some local authority workers to accept that the people who used their services *were* customers. I can remember some time-served local government employees being aghast when it was suggested that they made an effort to 'sell' their services – "We're public servants, not a street corner shop or Sainsbury's, you know!" It crossed my mind that very few servants spent their time telling their masters and mistresses what to do in the manner that many in local government did.

There were a number of occasions when I wondered whether some of the local government staff ever even considered the people they were supposed to be serving. Many of the documents they produced were simply impossible for the layman to understand. Some of my colleagues blamed the public and their inability to fill in forms properly, whereas the real problem was that the things had been largely written in 'officialese'.

Abstruse language was not limited to forms. I remember many years ago trying to read the so-called 'explanatory note' which fell out of the envelope containing the rate demand for the property I was living in. It was printed in incredibly small type, and looked as though reading it was going to be heavy going. I wondered if it had been designed this way on purpose, to prevent people trying to understand what was going on, and thereby to stop them being a nuisance by asking awkward questions. The notion that the property was subject to rates charged at so many shillings and pence in the pound was difficult enough to get my head around, but it came as a complete eye-opener to discover that I was living in a 'hereditament'. What on earth was one of those? After asking around I finally found out that it was an archaic word for 'property'.

This tendency to use language to confuse rather than enlighten still exists, and indeed is being encouraged and perpetrated for future use. I was listening recently to a radio documentary about fast-track graduates being turned out by one university as potential local government top managers. In the final part of their course they were attached to various councils to exercise their potential skills. The documentary's interviewer, who seemed to be enthused by the idea, asked a number of these bright, and doubtless bright-eyed, young things about the work they were doing in their attachments. One particular single-sentence reply was so long, and so full of fashionable governmental-type words – 'partnerships', 'out-reach', 'community', 'diversity', 'challenge', 'inclusiveness', 'going forward' and the like – that it was totally incomprehensible. Even the enthused interviewer was forced to ask the bright-eyed young thing in question what he actually meant. He seemed to struggle, and stumbled around in the verbiage. In a perverse kind of way, it was comforting to know that gobbledegook continues to flourish in public service.

The very role of public servant seemed to give rise to some curious attitudes towards the customers. Some good examples of this curiosity were to be found in our Local Taxation Department. In those days local authorities collected road tax and issued tax discs for cars. The department also dealt with other minor collection duties, including dog licences, which lingered on, I believe, until someone in Whitehall decided that the cost was so far in excess of the income that it wasn't worth it.

Every organisation has corners which could be described as 'sin bins' and in our case this was the Local Taxation Department. It seemed a number of the staff had been drafted in from other parts after being deemed surplus to requirements, or after allegedly being involved with misdemeanours. This, together with the fact that the work of the Department was humdrum and boring, meant that there was a splendid proliferation of jobsworths – much sticking to the rules, demotivation and boredom, which led to long faces and misery, much of which could only be dealt with by taking things out on the public.

Car-owners who wanted to buy their tax-disc in person were faced with a large hall off a separate entrance to County Hall which was furnished with a few tables and fewer chairs. At one end was a wide counter behind which was a raised floor which enabled the grim people who dispensed the licences to physically look down on their customers. Mentally they would have looked down on them anyway, but the increased height added an extra dimension which most collectors of tax seemed to relish. At busy times like the ends of months there were three queues which snaked around the hall. All moved at different speeds, and as was the case with old-fashioned Post Offices, it was impossible to guess which one to join for the quickest service. Actually, joining any of the queues was likely to feel like being in Purgatory, which didn't ease the temper of the transaction when the counter was finally reached.

To obtain a tax disc customers had to produce a completed application form, the vehicle log book, an insurance certificate,

an MOT test certificate and cash or a cheque for the right amount. After a period of time in Purgatory, the final arrival at the counter was not usually acknowledged, except with a curt "Documents, please". The papers were scrutinised, and if there was any shortcoming, this would be announced loudly – "Cheque's not signed!", "No MOT certificate" and so on. It was of no avail to produce a pen or fish in a bag or pocket for the missing document to make amends. The loud instruction "Back of the queue!" was given, followed by "Next!" So the miscreant customer had to retreat feeling like a naughty schoolchild, and was sentenced to another indefinite wait.

Curious attitudes existed in other places, too. I remember once asking a librarian why libraries weren't open when many people needed them.

"What do you mean?" she asked.

"Well, I think I'm fairly typical in that I work all week, go to the shops on Saturday, so Sunday is when I have most of my free time."

She drew herself up to her full height. "Librarians are human, too, you know, and need time off from work," she said, stonily. "Libraries have never opened on Sundays, and never will!"

I felt that I had committed an unforgivable heresy by even suggesting that the *status quo* could be challenged.

I can remember, too, the howls of wrath and anguish which emanated from some in the library service when someone had the audacity to suggest that, because so many requests were received for them, libraries should stock popular novels of the Mills and Boon variety. "Libraries aren't meant for that sort of stuff," came the cry from many of the professionals. "They are there to educate and improve people's minds and to promote *real* literature." With that style of thinking, I wonder what the response would have been then to *Fifty Shades of Grey*?

There were some aspects of the library service which were, however, excellent. There was a proud boast that, given time, a copy of almost any book could be obtained for a borrower. I don't think that this pledge extended to such things as the original folio editions of the works of Shakespeare, but it did work well for more ordinary tomes. I remember requesting a book dealing with some slightly obscure dimension of American local government which duly arrived after a few weeks bearing a rubber stamp on the fly-leaf reading 'Library of Congress, Washington'. Most impressive.

Not every one of the many thousands of volumes possessed by the county library was immediately accessible to every member of the public. Principal among these hard-to-get books were such historic erotic works as *The Perfumed Garden*, *The Kama Sutra* and *Lady Chatterley's Lover*. These were kept in a locked cabinet in the office of the county librarian, to which only a selected few had access, and were lent out only to people who wanted to read them for 'genuine purposes'. I wondered vaguely if someone had concocted a list of unacceptable purposes, and, if so, what these might be.

I had a colleague who applied for, and got, a very senior post in the library headquarters. I saw him not long after he started his new job and asked how things were going. "I know I've arrived," he said, with a huge grin. "I've been given a key to the mucky books cabinet."

Also at the library headquarters was the central reference library. This consisted of two or three rooms containing the more commonly used reference works, with plenty of space for the public to sit at tables and peruse them, plus what was known as 'the stack'. This was a massive set of steel shelves which were able to be moved tightly together by means of levers and small versions of ship's steering wheels to save space. The stack was used to store the older and less frequently used volumes. As far as I know, nobody ever got crushed between the heavy moving parts, so there must have been some safety device, but the stack was responsible for one accident I knew of. The reference librarian was a fine, down-to-earth fellow who had an immense knowledge of the works under his care.

I had to make a number of visits to the stack, and on one of them I noticed a large scab on the reference librarian's balding scalp. I commented that it looked painful.

"How did the injury happen?" I asked.

"I was working in here and a heavy book became dislodged from the top shelf and fell on my head."

We had by that time finished in the stack, and were emerging into the outside world of quietly seated seekers after knowledge.

"I bet you said something when it happened"

"Oh, yes. I said 'ferking bloody hell!' Oops! Sorry, ladies and gentlemen."

Which surely demonstrated that librarians were indeed human.

Not every member of the public thought local authorities were faceless and inhuman. At that time our Fire Brigade ran a fleet of fire engines most of which had bodies manufactured by John Dennis Coachbuilders of Guildford. These always-glistening machines had 'DENNIS' emblazoned in embossed shiny characters across the front of their cabs. A friend of mine who worked for the Fire Brigade told me they had once received a letter from a lady who congratulated them on presenting a delightfully human image by naming their fire engines. She had been out and about, and the fire engine named Dennis had passed her on the road.

I once had a conversation with a highways engineer about how his department worked out the priorities for roadworks in the county. The reply was very like the one I received in response to my much earlier enquiry about health centres.

"The professional engineers determine what needs to be done, and we inform the committee of progress," he said.

"Do you ever consult with the public?"

"Not directly. Usually the only time they get involved is when there is a public enquiry. After all, they elect the councillors to make decisions on their behalf."

This was by no means the only time that I had heard this argument for keeping the public at a distance and it seemed a little frail to me.

"Mind you," said the highways engineer. "The real reason why we don't ask the public what they want is that they might tell us, and that might conflict with what we tell them they need and what they are going to get."

There was also the case where an elderly member of the public had written to the Highways Department complaining that the street light outside her house was not working, and asking for it to be repaired quickly, because it illuminated her garden path and her front bedroom, thus saving her electricity. On a visit to the recipient's workplace on other matters, I noticed the reply, drafted by a more junior member of staff, on his desk, ready for the More Exalted One's signature. It was long, and astoundingly full of irrelevances, beginning with the information that what the complainant was referring to was technically termed an 'outage', dragging in a Highways Act (street lighting was for the benefit of road users and not to save private individuals' electricity), and that another agency – namely the electricity board – was responsible for dealing with outages. And all the member of the public wanted was for someone to change the bulb.

County Hall was a mile or so out of the town centre, and an interesting insight into what the public really thought about the Council was provided by a couple of bus conductors on the service which passed by on the main road. In those days many conductors used to call out the names of the stops, and as they approached County Hall one of them would always shout out "Butlins!" His colleague's cry was "The Kremlin!" I fancy that between them they might have identified the essential essence of the place. Incidentally, the "Butlins" man's humour extended further: when stopping outside the local police headquarters he would call out "Bluebottle Hotel!"

A splendid customer and council confrontation occurred at County Hall one morning when a furious middle-aged man burst through the main doors, shot past reception, stomped up a long corridor and burst into the office of the clerk of the council in an attempt to carry out a citizen's arrest. He was outraged at a council planning decision with which he disagreed – something to do with some trees. The clerk was flummoxed, and really didn't have much idea of what to do. The matter was finally sorted out after his secretary summoned help, and the police arrived to escort the protester off the premises. Strong words were exchanged, but no blood was spilled.

One of my favourite examples of customer service in local government happened during a visit to an old people's home. Sitting in comfortable isolation in the residents' lounge was a courteous and mild-mannered old lady – frail, but mobile. It was coming up to lunchtime, and a care assistant appeared.

"Come along, poppet, it's lunch time – can you go to the dining room?" she said, before going off to patronise someone else.

The mild-mannered frail old lady rose to her feet and looked me straight in the eye.

"If she calls me 'poppet' one more time I swear I'll wring her ferking neck!"

9

A BUNKER MENTALITY

In addition to its more mainstream activities, local government harboured some smaller corners of unexpected activity. When I first joined the council, something called Civil Defence still existed, an organisation dating back to just after World War II.

There to help out with emergencies such as floods and pestilence, it later became much more about saving our way of life should some aggressor choose to try to bomb the country out of existence. When I joined the county council the Cuban missile crisis of 1962 was still a recent memory and the Cold War rumbled along in the background for the whole of my time in local government. Emergency Officers came to be standard fixtures in big authorities. These worthies were generally retired military officers, many of whom clearly missed service life and their uniforms. They tended to appear in tweed jackets and cavalry twill trousers, and, somewhat worryingly, tended also to preface their pronouncements with the phrase "When there is another war" rather than with the slightly more optimistic "If there is another war". They were there to co-ordinate civil defence and the efforts of the emergency services: unfortunately for them, but fortunately for the rest of us, such problems were few and far between, so practically all their attention was paid to preparation. Manuals were produced and meetings were held.

County Hall was built at a time of atomic awareness, and the basement in one wing of the building was officially, but quietly, declared to be secure from any attack except a direct hit from a nuclear weapon. This was because there were many tons of reinforced concrete separating the bunker from the ground floor above it. One of the problems that occurred to me, hardly an expert in the field of nuclear warfare, was that, no matter how physically safe the basement might have been, the air supply was sucked in from the outside world and this would doubtless be tainted with radioactive dust if the big bang actually happened.

The idea was that in a time of nuclear emergency selected councillors and high-ranking council officials would be cocooned in the bunker to administer whatever remained of the county until it was safe to emerge. Having knowledge of some of the chosen few, I felt that their contributions towards stabilising the situation and returning things to normal might cause even more chaos.

I have already noted that my first days working for the council were not exactly busy, so when one of the retired brigadiers decided that a trained group of people was needed to provide practical help to the decision-makers in the bomb-proof basement, I put my name forward. In due course a twenty or so intrepid, or possibly bored, council officers assembled, and were told to report one afternoon a month to a room in the bunker for instruction. It was comforting to learn by implication that the retired military men weren't anticipating immediate Armageddon because one gathered that the monthly instruction afternoon was to be a fixture for the foreseeable future.

On reporting for duty, we found ourselves in a briefing room that looked vaguely familiar, thanks to our exposure to World War II films. The stark magnolia-painted walls grew out of a concrete floor upon which three rows of steel and canvas stackable chairs were arranged in front of a lectern. Various steel cupboards and filing cabinets, in khaki green, of course, were scattered around the walls, and behind the lectern was a projection screen and a pinboard exhibiting a large map of the county. The whole was lit by blindingly bright, unshaded fluorescent tubes (whose electricity supplies were, of course, ensured even if war came).

Two sets of tweed jackets and cavalry twill trousers appeared and introduced themselves, after which one of them took up position behind the lectern, not quite standing to attention, but close to it. This first afternoon was an introductory session, and we were regaled with the strategic background and possibilities for warfare and its aftermath in our area, accompanied by vigorous use of a long wooden pointer to indicate appropriate parts of the map. There was much talk of epicentres and fallout and refugees, and some slight reference to the imperative need for local administration to continue uninterrupted in post-nuclear chaos. I wondered in passing what the purposes of administering a devastated radioactive desert might be, but said nothing.

At our second meeting in the dungeon one of the tweed jackets called out names, followed by our allotted roles. I was to be a radio operator. Others were to become seekers after information about refugees, locators and procurers of rations, telephonists and despatch riders. The last immediately conjured up a vision in my mind of a World War II soldier riding a khaki motor-cycle equipped with panniers and one of those squashy triangular saddles balanced on a nest of coil springs. My vision was apparently shared by the man to whom this role had been assigned, because he immediately spoke up.

"I'm sorry, but I can't actually ride a motorbike."

"Don't worry," said Tweed Jacket. "We've advanced a bit since the war. You'll be able to use your car, and the county will pay you for your mileage."

The despatch rider was temporarily mollified, but became difficult again after one of the telephonists mentioned that an awful lot of telephone lines in the county were suspended above ground from poles.

"Surely a big explosion would cause the poles to fall and severe the wires," he pointed out. "And the telephone exchanges might be destroyed or damaged, too."

Tweed Jacket was equal to the argument. "You'll be pleased to know that we have considered these possibilities, and we shall be able to cope. After all, if the telephone system is out, we still have the roads and our despatch riders to convey information."

"In all the war films I've ever seen," said the despatch rider, "bombs have damaged roads and bridges as well as telephone wires. How do I know that I'm not going to finish up driving into a crater?"

"That shouldn't happen. The engineers will have road repairs at the top of their priority list."

From his face, the despatch rider was clearly unconvinced. I was not terribly convinced either. With my radio operator's hat on,

I recalled a news item I had read some months previously which revealed that after a nuclear test in the Pacific there had been a radio blackout lasting for quite a time which spanned many miles from the centre of the explosion. I decided to keep my powder dry, reserving any observation I might have for another time.

As it happened, that other time never occurred. After a couple more meetings, each with a dwindling number of attendees, the project quietly disappeared into the ether. I confess that I didn't weep bitter tears.

On the subject of radio operation, I later learned that when the building containing the bomb-proof basement was first occupied, an eager group of Emergency staff asked a locally stationed army group to test out the feasibility of radio contact with the bunker. Starting several miles away, the army sent out test signals while the men in the basement stood by the receiver in anticipation. Silence. An Emergency person ascended from the bowels and, using a walkie-talkie radio, contacted the army group and asked them to move a little closer. Silence again. Another walkie-talkie conversation along the same lines ensued. Still more silence. The whole process was repeated again and again until at long last a signal was received in the basement. The only problem was that when this happened the army signallers were right outside the main door of the building. The bunker may or may not have been bomb-proof, but sure as hell it was radio-proof.

'Local Government in Emergency' didn't go away. Every now and then Emergency staff went to Important Meetings inside and outside the county, with senior civil servants, military staff and politicians. There were also occasional exercises designed to test systems or readiness.

We were a pretty rural county, and it was the major centres of population which might reasonably be supposed to be the first targets of nuclear attack. The feeling was that even if we weren't directly involved in the first bouts of mayhem, we would be a natural destination for evacuees and those migrating from stricken cities. I remember that, much later than my brush with the plans for post-attack strategy, a couple of colleagues were co-opted to assist in an exercise which was designed to test whether systems for dealing with this influx of human hordes would work. Not only was the county council involved, but all the district councils in the county were in on the exercise, too.

When they returned from the bunker after the exercise I asked how things had gone.

"If ever the balloon does go up I think things will work all right, providing that those fleeing from the nuclear holocaust come at the right time," said my colleague.

"What do you mean?"

"Well, at about twelve thirty we received information in the exercise scenario that several hundred evacuees were heading for the north of the county. We worked out which of the district councils would be best able to cope with the number, and I phoned the emergency team there. After rather a long time an unexpected voice answered the phone, and I asked if I was speaking to a member of the emergency team. 'Oh, no,' said the unexpected voice, 'this is main reception. The emergency team have transferred their phones to me because they've all gone for lunch.'"

10

ON THE FIDDLE

The convoluted nature of big organisations such as local authorities means that they offer an infinite variety of possibilities for playing the system and, in short, nicking things.

Vince introduced me to a more-or-less-honest way of acquiring things, which he did not suggest for any personal gain, but simply as a system for obtaining stuff to be used at work. He described the method – "Without anyone noticing, move the desired object from its usual position to another place where it is still clearly in view. Leave it for a few days. If it resumes its previous position that means that it is still in use, and should probably be left alone. If, however, the object remains in the position to which you moved it, move it once more, but this time to a less visible place, again making sure that you are not observed. Wait a few more days, go through the process again, and actually hide the item. Wait another few days, and then, if the object is still there in the place you hid it, take possession of it."

Vince had once been an internal auditor. Public bodies have a superficial obsession with 'public money', and can become paranoid about finding out the fate of the last penny and ensuring that staff are not bending the rules or infringing financial regulations. To this end they have fleets of internal auditors to check on the honesty of employees. Many of these audit people seem to start from the premise that all human beings are basically dishonest ne'er-do-wells who will do anything to thieve and steal from and otherwise screw their employers. This attitude is not too good for morale in a type of organisation which does not spend an enormous amount of effort loving and trusting those who work for it anyway.

Vince, however, was not of this ilk: he actually liked people and tried to understand them. Whenever a story of some incredibly complicated fraud emerged, Vince would shake his head wisely and say something like "When will people ever learn that the most successful way to steal is the straight pinch with a reasonable alibi, if necessary". He introduced me to the audit expression 'teeming and lading', which I gathered meant constantly moving money or goods about to hide theft. He maintained that one of the tell-tale signs of someone doing this was that they were always in their workplace, were never sick and only took short holidays. This was to ensure that no-one else would get chance to stick their noses in and become suspicious about what was going on.

Vince liked to regale me with stories about his days in audit. He talked about auditing school canteens during the days of food rationing, where temptation understandably put a strain on maintaining the correct food-stocks. In a catering business there is always room for a bit of slippage, but from time to time the discrepancy was so large that a real investigation had to happen. On one occasion, the audit team discovered that canteen assistants were taking butter home in their bras. Bearing in mind that this was butter from an industrial-sized block and needed wrapping, I couldn't help wondering what state it was in when they got it home.

Vince also entertained me with a tale of an audit at the county's agricultural college. Here there were many opportunities for pinching things, so periodically there was much weighing of vegetables, and counting of equipment and livestock. Adding up the number of tractors and other machines was doubtless worthwhile, as were such activities as dipping diesel tanks to check the fuel level, but working through a stockpile of carrots with some weighing scales was probably one of the more time-wasting chores. Pigs and cows could be counted relatively easily, but calculating the number of free-range chickens in a large flock running around a field was a different matter. The auditor in charge was not, however, to be deterred.

He and his assistant got hold of some portable fencing hurdles which they set up in a rough funnel-shape which cut off one corner of the field. The idea was that the assistant would drive the chickens into the wide part of the funnel where they would work their way to the hurdle at its neck, where the senior auditor would count them as they hopped over the fence. All this might have been all right in theory, but anyone who knew anything about chickens would have seen a major flaw. What happened was this. At the beginning everything worked as planned. The assistant started shooing the chickens, which dutifully entered the funnel, where they milled around for a while. As the funnel became more crowded they began to look for a way out and one hopped onto the top of the end hurdle, exactly as required. The senior auditor was delighted, and duly put a tick on his clipboard. Then two more chickens hopped up, and were ticked, then half a dozen, then twenty or so, and then a positive tidal wave of squawking and frenetic birds in numbers impossible to calculate engulfed the hurdle. The auditors gave up and went away to count something else.

We often talked about fiddles we had heard about, if for no other reason than grudging admiration of human ingenuity.

A colleague who started his local government life as a trainee auditor claimed that as part of his traineeship he'd had to spend a sunny summer, with the cricket commentary playing softly on his transistor radio, lying on his stomach, concealed by riverside reeds and grasses, while he watched through binoculars an employee whose job was issuing tickets to motorists to enable them to use a stretch of toll road on the opposite bank of the river. The council had inherited the road and the employee from the previous owners, British Railways, and it was suspected that the keeper of the toll road was pocketing a slice of the income. Unfortunately, the keeper of the toll road spent a lot of time with his back to the binoculars or in his little hut, and nothing could be pinned on him. My colleague enjoyed being paid for keeping his cricket knowledge up-to-date, though.

Another colleague, with a background in railway work, reckoned that local government was not nearly such a fertile place for fiddling as the railway was. He had started as a junior at a moderately sized station and advised us to be careful if we visited a booking office where there was a doormat, apparently for passengers' convenience, directly below the window where the tickets were issued. He told us that a common wheeze was for booking clerks to be apparently deeply caught up in administrative duties which prevented them from serving potential passengers promptly. As train time approached, and people in the queue became uneasy, the clerk would leap to the window apologising profusely and serve everyone quickly. The trick was to give change using as many coins as possible, and people in their haste would scoop it up without counting it. Any coins which they dropped would land on the doormat without a sound. After the train departed, the booking clerk would emerge from the office and gather up the dropped coins.

The ex-railway colleague also told us of the occasional agreements between booking clerks and ticket collectors about platform tickets, which at that time were sold to people who wanted to go onto the platforms, but not to travel. The booking clerk would issue the ticket, but not date-stamp it. When the person left the platform, the ticket was collected and returned to the booking office for re-issue: the resulting cash was divided two ways. With each ticket worth a penny it seemed a lot of work for a modest reward, but then again the cheaper sort of beer was only about eighteen platform tickets a pint, so at a reasonably busy station, it might have been worth it.

Most big organisations, particularly in the public sector, seemed to believe that their staff were lazy and untrustworthy, and so they designed systems to ensure that people didn't take them for a ride. This gave rise to time-consuming and top-heavy practices. One of my favourite examples of this was the travel claim.

All employees who were *bona fide* travellers while going about the county council's business had to fill in a form at the end of each month to claim their expenses. I was always slightly tickled by the fact that after I completed the form:

    1.   I signed it off as an accurate record of expenses incurred

2. My manager signed it off also, thus endorsing my honesty
3. The departmental head signed it off to endorse my manager's view of my honesty
4. The departmental finance clerk signed it off after they had inserted the expenditure code
5. Someone in the treasurer's department scrutinised the form to ensure that I had claimed the right rate for the right things.

I came to the conclusion that you could tell exactly what an organisation thought about its employees by how they dealt with expense forms: the longer the chain of signing and counter-signing, from the time the form was filled in to the time it was eventually filed, the less trusting was the employer.

Every now and then an internal auditor would appear with a batch of old claim forms to check that the trips made coincided with my diary record of appointments and events. People who were not good at keeping diaries tended to have a miserable time. They were regularly pilloried by the auditors, who sometimes made phone calls to the places allegedly visited to check that the person really had been there on the stated date at the stated time (the latter was, of course, important because of meal allowances).

Arithmetic and honesty were not the only things to be checked. Dear old Archie, in the first county council office I worked in, spent a lot of time and effort checking routes and mileages with Ordnance Survey maps and a measuring device which was affectionately known as 'Archie's wheel', and which was considered to be the fount of ultimate accuracy as applied to travel claims. If Archie smelt even a hint of a rat about a claimed distance he would mutter "Time for the bloody wheel", and with due ceremony out it would come, accompanied by the appropriate map. When victorious in discovering a wrong mileage, Archie would mutter "They must think that we're ferking stupid and that we came up on the last down train!" – an observation which I found as opaque as any Russian proverb.

At that time the higher echelons of staff were allowed to travel first class when using the train for business. A very senior colleague told me how, when he'd worked for another county council, it was common practice to buy a second class ticket but claim on expenses for first class. He thought he'd try this out for himself, despite a few moral qualms. Standing on the platform for the London train, with his second class ticket ensconced in his wallet, he was horrified to see his boss, the clerk of the council, ploughing energetically through the throng of waiting travellers, obviously heading his way.

"Glad I've seen you," said the boss. "Going to London? Good. It will give us a chance to talk about the spec for that new computer." The train arrived, and the boss led the way into a first class carriage. The very senior colleague participated little in the conversation that ensued, because as a regular traveller to London he knew there was always a ticket inspection en route. With that 'you've been found out' sinking feeling in the pit of his stomach, he spent the journey wrestling with how he would handle the absence of a first class ticket, what story he would tell the ticket inspector, and how me might justify his second class status to the clerk of the council.

The train galloped on its way, putting the miles to London behind it. My very senior colleague interjected odd, but un-thought-through comments and observations about the proposed new computer into the conversation, constantly wondering whether a trip to the toilet at the appropriate time might provide him with a get-out-of-jail-free card. A major problem was that the carriage was of the once-fashionable variety with compartments and a side corridor, and he wouldn't be able to see the ticket inspector coming.

After an hour and twenty minutes or so of misery, my very senior colleague became dimly aware that the train was slowing down among the backs of tenement buildings he recognised as being not far from the terminus, and to his intense relief it pottered into its destination a few minutes later. For once, and exceptionally, there had been no ticket inspection on the train. He bade farewell to the boss, who had not even seemed to notice that the conversation had been a little one-sided, and vowed there and then that he would never, ever, get involved in any kind of fiddle again.

Would that there had been more like him.

One of the classics of fiddling is the invention of ghost members of staff. With the right kind of safeguards in position this is not terribly easy in the average organisation, but if the fiddlers are in the right place it is feasible.

We had a bright, personable young man who was a popular member of the payroll section. Anyone less liable to be involved in fraud would have been hard to imagine, or so everyone thought. But he had an unscrupulous mate who was a teacher at a school in the county, who persuaded him to become involved in a scam which would benefit them both. Between them, they invented an imaginary teacher. The payroll man looked after the setting up of the records and the business of payment, and his teaching friend looked after the other end of the scheme with a bank account for the non-existent person. The thing went on for over a year, until someone noticed that spending on the school's staffing budget didn't seem quite right.

The personable young man duly confessed. When the teacher friend had his collar felt he denied everything at first, but when he finally did own up was vitriolic, and threatened his friend with all kinds of retribution. In this case there seemed to be little honour among thieves.

An interesting variation on this theme happened when a headteacher of a moderately sized primary school invented a number of ghost pupils. At first glance this could have seemed a rather altruistic act, designed to enhance the amount the school could spend on its real pupils, but it soon came to light that the head had invented a way of siphoning off the surplus for his own ends. Justice was duly done. He went to languish in jail.

Money wasn't the only thing that people tried to get their hands on illegitimately. Most of us have made off with the odd pen or pencil from our workplaces. In fact, at this very moment I have one on the desk in front of me inscribed with the name of one of my former employers, and I take this opportunity of apologising profusely to Imperial Chemical Industries. During my time in local government I heard of various pieces of equipment, some of them quite large, going missing without trace, but a better fiddle was to use them for one's own profit. We once had a foreman of a roads gang who for years ran a private plant-hire business at evenings and weekends using county council equipment.

Time was another commodity open to theft, though to be perfectly fair to local government I have to admit that I learned to skive seriously while I worked in the private sector. My very first job was in a production plant employing around two thousand people, and I pretty soon discovered that setting off from my office after muttering something about visiting a couple of other departments, and carrying with me a couple of important-looking files and a preoccupied expression, I could wander around for long periods completely unchallenged. I honed the art-form at various other workplaces particularly those which offered maximum tedium and poor reward, but was still unprepared for the immense skiving possibilities offered by a large county council.

In my earliest position in the Health Department I spent a great deal of time socialising and making my presence known to the opposite sex, and later I'll tell you about how I discovered the uses to which the dim recesses of the storage area in the roof of County Hall could be put. Over the years, too, I spent many hours of public service time discussing television, sport, pastimes, current affairs, holidays, cars, love-life and so on with colleagues in other extreme reaches of the building.

Once I became the holder of a job which involved visiting outlying parts of the empire, the opportunities for stealing time were greatly multiplied. Slow meanders over circuitous routes through the summer countryside before or after meetings were a particular freedom, and were virtually undiscoverable if the mileage subsequently claimed was for the most direct route. Extensions to legitimate visits in order to rendezvous with colleagues not seen for a while, or detours to places 'just to see how things are going', were routine.

Cricket was sometimes the cause of my straying from the straight and narrow. Quick dashes to the car park to spend a few minutes listening to *Test Match Special* on the car radio were not unusual and, much later, I'd go with the cricket-mad colleague (he of road-toll spying fame) to spend a couple of hours at the county cricket ground – if we had a meeting that had taken us in roughly the right direction, of course.

Many people have always arrived for work a little late or departed early, but when formality sets in, curiosities emerge. In common with many other organisations, the county council eventually introduced flexible working for many of its employees. Trust was not at the top of the agenda, however, so time clocks were introduced. There was a touch of wryness about this, for at same the time some of the council's workshop staff were threatening to strike if the time clocks weren't removed from their workplace, while the office workers' union was threatening to strike if time clocks were not introduced!

Just like the work study stop-watches, these time clocks subdivided hours into decimal minutes – one hundred to the hour – for ease of calculation. Every Monday, all members of staff added up the figures on their clock cards and calculated their hours for the previous week. The cards were handed in to the administration office where (wait for it) the arithmetic on all of them was checked. This used to take a jobsworth at least a couple of hours, and thereafter this worthy would wander around the department informing people that they had made a mistake and that an amended figure for hours carried forward would have to be entered on their card for the current week. Most of the mistakes involved very small numbers of decimal minutes, but nevertheless this little exercise would occupy the jobsworth for a further hour or so. It struck me as a rather curious use of time. A similar rigmarole was indulged in for collecting small numbers of pennies owed for personal telephone calls. Never mind the real priorities – what about that sixpence you owe?

I notice that in many places there is an increasing army of people, who, possibly in self-defence, are busy being busy. I'm still deeply suspicious when people tell me that they don't have time or resources to do what they should be doing. It's not what you haven't got that gets in the way of success, it's what you do, or don't do, with what you *have* got that is mostly the problem. But that's jobsworths for you.

11

WE'RE HERE BECAUSE WE'RE HERE

Intimacy with an intricate organisation such as a local authority and the people in it means that aspects of human nature and behaviour become more clearly noticed, and in my time we had our fair share of obsessives, eccentrics and the blinkered boring mindless.

Where to start? Well, the office workers' trade union representative provided an interesting service for the female staff at County Hall. Being good public sector furniture, the desks and tables – most of them custom-built for the opening of the building – were made of wood. A problem with good old-fashioned wood is that splinters occur, and quite frequently female staff snagged their tights on them. The union man always had a ready supply of tights in several sizes and shades available free. I'm sure that this went somewhat beyond the requirements of his union role, but I didn't altogether subscribe to the view of one or two of my more scurrilous colleagues that he really ought to have gone the whole way and offered a free fitting service.

One of the products which local authority bureaucracies are particularly good at producing is paperwork, and I'm not sure that the quantity has substantially diminished in the present age of electronic distribution and storage of information, in spite of the fact that we were promised the paperless office many years ago. Certainly in my time at the council, paper records existed by the ton, and when they reached a particular age they needed to be put into storage. It was fortunate that County Hall had a huge attic, and this was largely given over to the storage of old files. Each department had its own area – trespassing on the territory of other realms was severely frowned upon – and this meant that there was a series of cages, each full of files, creating a dimly lit maze in which it was perfectly possible to get lost for hours on the pretext of doing important things. The attic was mainly occupied by the odd individual who was trying to kill time before going to lunch or going home, or by one or two poor clerical assistants wading their way through dusty heaps for something that had been misfiled a dozen years previously by someone who didn't much care where they put it as long as it was out of the way.

Work was not the only reason for visiting the maze. In a building containing upwards of nine hundred people, it was inevitable that relationships which embraced more than work should happen. If the need for the occasional clandestine embrace occurred, the roof space provided a convenient, if somewhat unromantic, venue. It was most in demand around the festive season when there had been a departmental Christmas lunch or two. Then the maze might become more populated than usual, with the darker corners mostly in demand.

There was also a goods lift with a sliding lattice gate which not only serviced all four floors of the building, but the roof space as well, and which was regarded by some as a jolly handy and creative spot for a bit of rapid nookie. If the gate was opened slightly between floors, the lift stopped its stately progress up or down, and what was going on inside was invisible because of solid concertina doors on the 'landward' side on each floor. You had to be quick, though, because there were a number of genuine users who got fed up with the lift's non-appearance, and who went searching for its whereabouts, climbing stairs and peering through the small window in the doors. It was possible to switch off the internal light off, but previous experience had taught one or two of the seekers to shine torches through the small windows to see what the problem was.

The man responsible for the day-to-day running of County Hall seemed to have an obsession about goings-on in the roof space, and was a frequent visitor to the area, which he patrolled thoroughly and silently, sometimes frightening the hunters of elderly documents. The less kind, when remarking upon this apparent obsession, even suggested that he purposely bought soft-soled shoes so that his presence was less likely to be detected. And when it came to misuse of the goods lift, because the flawless operation of the County Hall lifts was part of his responsibility and any apparent malfunction had to be reported to him, he naturally revelled in being one of the principal torch users.

One of the people I worked with over the years was the deputy computer manager. He was a placid and intelligent man, and, with hindsight, I think that his particular obsession was the style of the era he lived in – its sartorial flamboyance, colour and style, its music and its *laissez faire* approach to some aspects of life. When I first met him in the late 1960s, he bore more than a passing resemblance to the actor Peter Wyngarde who played Jason King in the popular TV series *Department S*, in which the main characters spent a lot of time in quality cars on picturesque roads by the Mediterranean, dealing with hush-hush intelligence problems. The deputy computer manager claimed, though, that he didn't watch much television and was more interested in the cinema. He said that one of the most amazing experiences of his life was watching the film *Easy Rider*, but I believe that what he was smoking at the time might have contributed to some of the amazement. He always smoked tobacco when at work, but I couldn't help wondering sometimes if his pleasant placidity was the result of sometimes being a bit stoned when off-duty.

Because the computer section was a new entity populated by young members of staff, many of whom were unencumbered by traditional local government attitudes, there was much camaraderie. Some of this manifested itself in regular parties. I was happy to be regularly invited to these, but I particularly recall one which took place at the deputy computer manager's house. This gathering was all that a late 1960s event should have been, and for me was not only notable for the colourful clothing on show, the quantities of alcohol consumed, the various goings-on that took place and the scent marijuana, but mainly because I was introduced to the music of Jimi Hendrix. My musical taste at that time was catholic – a melange of pop and classical, with an enthusiasm for trad jazz. But Hendrix's skill with the electric guitar, and the kinds of sounds that he produced, were the entry into an amazing and exciting musical world for me.

Smoking in the workplace was very much the norm: in fact, if you weren't a smoker, you were unusual. Cigarettes were more common than pipes, but there were some pipe smokers, and there is no denying that a pipe lent a certain air of authority. I had one such colleague who had this air anyway, and his pipe, which, if he wasn't smoking it, always resided on the outer ledge of a rather grand stainless steel ashtray, simply emphasised it. He had retired from the Royal Air Force with the rank of Wing Commander, and after flying a desk for a while in the Air Ministry, had migrated to our local authority to while away a few years before retirement. Knocking on office doors before entry was dying out as a regular part of workplace courtesy, but when visiting this gentleman's realm knocking still somehow seemed to be the proper thing to do.

After the knock came the invitation to enter. I was usually there to seek advice or to bounce ideas off him for whatever project I was working on. His response was always helpful, but a set series of actions had to be undertaken first. He would listen, apparently carefully, then emit an interested "hmmm", and look out of the window while his right hand automatically picked up the pipe. He would then peer into it, tamp the contents down with a device especially made for this, put the pipe in his mouth, light it, and take a deep breath before exhaling a fragrant cloud of blue smoke. Only then would he answer my query. And do you know, it didn't matter at all what the answer was – you just knew that whatever was said would be a considered and deeply thought-through nugget of experience and opinion. Demonstrating the law of unintended consequences, the move towards a non-smoking world has destroyed a mechanism which, it seems, greatly enhanced the human thought process.

There was another pipe-smoking man in the department who once upon a time, perhaps a little unfashionably for those days, decided that tobacco was a most unhealthy substance. He didn't, however, want to give up smoking and so resorted to a commercially produced mixture of various cured plants, of which coltsfoot was one, which was claimed by its makers to be much more healthy, and aromatic to boot. This stuff came in large quantities in polythene bags and looked like dried and crushed garden waste, which, of course, it probably was. The large quantities were required because its combustion rate was much higher than that of tobacco; scarcely had the pipe been filled and lit, than a top up was needed. 'Aromatic' may have been the manufacturer's description, but those in the vicinity of its smoker tended to use words like 'evil', and to cough rather a lot when inhaling the bonfire-like fumes. After a short while the man was banished to the empty office next door. Even then we were not fully isolated from the noxious vapours, which crept under the door and worked their way relentlessly down the corridor for several yards, to insinuate themselves into every opening that they found. Mercifully for all concerned, probably including himself, the pipe smoker fairly quickly reconsidered his choice and returned to tobacco.

The early 1970s was the period which ushered in the era of the local government 'non-job'. The era is still with us, and continues to spawn some curious job titles, and even whole organisations such as the unloved and largely purposeless late regional assemblies. Perhaps the trend started with a change in social attitudes, sometimes supported by what at the time seemed to be a positive plethora of legislation. Some of the non-jobs were the children of things which started vaguely legitimately, but which later morphed into reflections of political correctness or flavours of the month. Change and more sensitivity were certainly needed but as in all things, when the public sector gets hold of an idea, particularly one which could be useful in terms of power, job numbers and salary grades, obsession sets in. Things become self-fulfilling prophecies and self-perpetuating systems, and rapidly create approaches which amount to "We're here because we're here, because we're here", within no time at all becoming immoveable parts of the *status quo* with lives of their own. The later episode of the television series *Yes, Minister* which featured a new hospital, fully staffed and running faultlessly, but totally free of patients, was not far from the truth.

We acquired our fair share of jobs which had no immediate purpose, but which were held by hard-working people who were obsessively and fiercely protective of what they did, and who were very busy doing whatever it was. I remember suggesting to one of my colleagues who occupied such a job in some curious corner of the organisation that if quite a few of us were wiped from the face of the earth, nobody would actually notice. He was horrified, and told me in no uncertain terms that I was wrong, that we were desperately important to the fabric of society and that we were bringing real benefit to the communities we served.

One day I was discussing with a high-up person in the Education Department the creation of a new senior position. At the time the education hierarchy was complaining loud, long and bitterly about the shortage of resources and how impossible it was to provide a quality service.

"What might the prime purpose of this proposed position be?" I asked, perhaps naively.

"Well" replied the high up person, "we haven't quite made our minds up yet, but we'll decide as soon as we see what kind of person we have appointed."

There is no greater jobsworth than a small-minded individual put in charge of something minor which they feel they own, and which enables them to flex their power muscles. The memory of one such has truly stayed with me for years. He was the Lord of the Stationery Cupboard in a divisional police headquarters.

The Lord of the Cupboard was a civilian who had come into the job after serving his time as a constable. As might be expected after a life of discipline, conformity and doing things the 'proper' way, he brought those qualities which had made him an eternally bottom-end beat bobby for all those years to his new role as a bottom-end clerical assistant. An important part of his job was stocking, supervising and ensuring the smooth operation of the stationery cupboard. When he took up his post he dreamt up, without reference to anyone, a number of his own rules, including one which dictated that the cupboard would only be opened between nine o'clock and ten o'clock in the morning. This meant that during this hour there was a queue of people of all ranks, from typists to divisional commanders, seeking items, and nobody ever queried why the cupboard was only open for one hour a day. Perhaps the Lord of the Cupboard was getting his own back on his senior uniformed colleagues after many years of being downtrodden.

My favourite of his rules concerned the issue of pencils. He had arbitrarily decided that pencils were useable until they were only one and a half inches long. An interesting use of constabulary time was the deliberate measuring of pencil stubs when a new one was required, and the subsequent deliberation as to whether the length made it eligible for replacement. Pencils which were even a quarter of an inch too long were referred back to their owners for further use, and on no account was a new pencil issued unless the stub of an existing one was offered. I learned that the Lord of the Cupboard's holidays and time off were greatly looked forward to.

At times, certain council staff felt themselves to be indispensible. There was once a minor strike by social workers. I can't remember the reason for the action and in fact the whole thing was over in a few days. Some of the strikers were incredulous, and even upset, that no-one had actually died or become worse off as a result of having no social work assistance while the strike was on.

All professions seem to have their own idiosyncratic curiosities. Speak to any librarian, certainly of the old school, and they will confirm that when putting books on shelves, regardless of the size of the volumes, all the spines should be neatly lined up half an inch from the edge of the shelf. Nothing used to aggravate librarians more than some wretched unthinking member of the public having the temerity to remove or replace books so that the beautiful symmetry of the line of spines was destroyed, and in many instances librarians would occupy their slacker moments visiting the shelves and reinstating the military precision, sometimes accompanying their efforts with a little quiet sighing and tutting.

Once, when I was talking to a quantity surveyor in our architects department, he spent a long time bemoaning the falling standards in his profession. His beef was with the production of 'bills of quantities' by computer.

"In the old days," he said, "when all the quantities were

typed out they were so neat, and we bound them beautifully. Now all we get are heaps of printouts on continuous stationery, and they look like any other computer printouts – just lines of type, all in capital letters. It's so hard to have any pride in them."

"Ichabod, Ichabod, for the glory is departed!" I muttered, under my breath.

Engineers and accounts always conducted meetings seated around a conference table, but many social workers and some educationalists preferred simply to put their chairs into a circle. This was, I think, supposed to create a barrier-free environment in which openness could flourish, but in reality was quite uncomfortable. It is uncommonly difficult to accommodate piles of papers and files in these kinds of get-togethers with nothing except the floor to put them on, and I, as a more common kind of mortal, never felt completely at ease. I remember one senior educationalist observing to me after one of these kinds of gatherings which had been singularly unproductive and where people had been very uninvolved: "Do you know, when we sit round like this and people aren't responding I have a strong desire to ask everyone present to hold hands and get in touch with the living!"

Some of the ways in which people used their employment to pursue their own interests never ceased to amaze me. We had one or two people who spent their whole working lives organising the sports and social club. They may have been employed to do apparently important jobs for the council, but the really important things to them were the team for the next cricket match or the state of the departmental volleyball league or the details of the next dance. There was one man who spent much of his time in the office organising staff trips to concerts and theatre shows. Without doubt, though, the top prize for the most wacky use of the organisation's time should have been awarded to the man in the Highway Engineers' department who, I was reliably informed, spent many happy hours designing, purely for his own enjoyment, totally impossible and impractical underground railway systems for the county, when he should have been doing important highways things. It was well known that he had been doing this for years, but no-one ever reprimanded him.

Thinking of personalised approaches to how work is done leads me to recall a time-served employee who for years did his bit to minimise the mountain of paper that characterised local government. He had a table in his office upon which he stacked his incoming mail in neat piles, one for every week. The table accommodated about twelve piles. The man in question had a work philosophy which went like this: "I am not going to reply to any incoming letter or memo, because the vast majority of the stuff is unimportant or meaningless. If something *is* important, and I really have to be involved with it, the other people will ring me or pay me a visit. I shall know pretty much where the original piece of paper is, because of my weekly piles, and it can then be dealt with." His first act every Monday morning was to place his empty litter bin by the oldest pile, sweep it majestically in, and then move all the other piles up one place, thus creating space for the current week's incoming heap. As far as I know, he never got caught. When I first heard about this I was appalled, but as time went on, I became more and more convinced that there was something to be said for his system.

In truth, is always advisable to be wary about first impressions. The sober-suited, upright and unsmiling people in the Education Department, for example, didn't seem to have a lot of fun. Education was a serious subject, not to be dealt with by the light-hearted and this rather puritanical attitude seemed to stem from the top, and permeated the ranks of the less exalted employees. I remember being surprised by my encounter with one rather senior administrator, renowned for his rather taciturn manner. While I was talking, he had glanced at his watch a couple of times.

"Sorry – am I getting in the way of another appointment?" I asked.

"Oh, no," he said. "It's just that the lads are playing at home tonight, and I want to be away promptly. I never miss a match, you know."

"I hadn't got you down as a football fan."

"Not so much a fan, more a fanatic. I've supported the local team since I was a lad. I know they're not doing too well in the league at the moment, but they still have a dedicated core of fans rooting for them. I'm one of them. You should see me on the terraces – I turn into an animal!"

It took some time for me to adjust my image of the man, and in fact it put something of a strain on my imagination to see him in this new light.

Local authorities have always depended upon bureaucratic structures and in those days tended to have many tiers of management. This meant that 'position power' was usually far more important than individual personalities. When I first started my career in public service there were occasions when I unwittingly infringed the protocol by telephoning or speaking directly to people I needed to deal with in other parts of the organisation. I was reminded gently by those who knew about such things that I should really have spoken about the matter to my section head, who would then get in touch with his opposite number in the department in question either to seek permission to allow me to deal person-to-person, or to get the person's section head to seek the answer to the query on my behalf and transmit it to my section head for eventual onward transmission to me.

I mentioned earlier the oddity of allowing only the chief's name as the signatory of correspondence. Many were the chiefs whose last (and expensive) hour or two of their working day was occupied by the signing of letters originating from all corners of their department. The chiefs could only have had a pretty hazy knowledge about most of it as the correspondence was on such a wide range of topics. It was considered important that the process was carried out, however, just in case someone was dealing with something they shouldn't or was trying to steal some power.

To be fair, public service was not alone in its careful protection of the status of top staff. I can remember being a little bemused – and amused –when my bank sent me letters which had at their foot the admonishment "All correspondence to be addressed to the Manager". It was as if the manager knew every one of their hundreds or thousands of customers personally. Either that or, in the manner of local government, there was a view that lesser mortals on the payroll were stupid or untrustworthy and should not be let loose on those outside the business.

Sometimes, to save time, part of the labour of signing had to be delegated, but the chief's name was still always there. In one or two departments a mark of status was the issuing of rubber stamps which gave an imprint of the boss's signature. These were carefully distributed only to those who, as it were, sat at God's right hand, and who could be trusted not to abuse the privilege vested in them that the possession of the stamp implied. I did hear of one example of transgression where the rubber stamp had been used to sign a letter relating to some supposedly high-level financial transaction which had not been referred to God, and of which, when it came to light, God did not approve. The miscreant was summoned and given a good dressing down. His stamp was confiscated.

For most of us, however, the delegation of signing powers simply allowed the chief's name to be written at the foot of standard letters. The regimen did slacken slightly as time went on, and we had an issue of a new form of letterhead which had the chief's title and name, followed by yards of initials indicating qualifications and membership of professional bodies, emblazoned at its head, and which was allowed to carry the signature of a slightly more junior manager at its foot. Somewhere alongside that part where the date was intended to appear was also a little note which said 'If telephoning please ask for ---------------- on extension-------' It was thus quite possible that the unsuspecting recipient of the letter would have a choice of three names to write to in reply. I was tickled when I was negotiating a visit to a nationally renowned organisation to look at aspects of how they worked, to receive a reply from their general manager thanking us all for our interest, and asking that we should let him know which of us would be visiting!

On another occasion I received a letter confirming some arrangements made through a number of telephone conversations.

The letter started with the greeting 'Dear Malcolm'. This was not unreasonable, since we had developed a friendly relationship during our long chats. The letter, of course, went through the 'morning prayers' process in the chief's office, and eventually arrived on my desk with a ring drawn around the 'Dear Malcolm' and a note written alongside which read 'personality cult!' When I asked what the problem was, I was told that it was not considered healthy for local authority employees to develop first-name relationships with people they were dealing with outside the organisation.

This obsession with status was greatly, if slowly, eroded over the years by the increasing use of the telephone and has, hopefully, been driven almost to extinction by the universal use of e-mail.

There were other signs of status-obsession, such as the use of miniature sets of 'traffic lights' outside the higher-ups in the Education Department. If you wanted an audience with the deity within, you knocked at the door and the deity pushed a button accordingly. A green light was an invitation to enter; a yellow light meant "I'm too busy for your less-than-important contribution at the moment, but hang around and I'll give you a green when I'm ready"; the red light meant "I'm utterly tied up. Go Away." I was always tickled to see high-ranking people who'd been given a yellow, kicking their expensive heels, sometimes for quite long periods, in the corridors outside the deities' domains.

Respect for seniority was treasured in some quarters, and many held the view that 'respect' automatically came, like an overcoat, with the salary grade and job title. I often heard people say "They can't speak to me like that – I'm a principal officer". A slightly different approach was relayed to me by a member of a Fire Service in another county, where the mantra among the top brass was "You respect the position, not the person". This seemed to suggest to me that any idiot could be in charge as long as they were wearing the right insignia on their uniform – and judging from my experience of some of these people at the top, quite a few idiots did get to be in charge.

For our chief highways engineer, Martin Halford, status was

the be-all-and-end-all. He had worked his way up from relatively humble beginnings, and placed great store on his progress. There was no great harm in that, but his advance was accompanied by some curious attitudes in the way he dealt with others. To show his superiority, he would regularly bawl out members of his staff in important meetings where people from other places were in attendance, and had the reputation of being something of a tyrant. Most people in his department tended to keep out of his way unless they couldn't help it. He was aggravated beyond measure when one of his sub-managers who looked after the roads in a particularly difficult geographical area was awarded an OBE for his efforts over the years in keeping the highways in his patch open in severe winter weather.

The chief clearly thought that, because he was in overall charge, the award should have come to him. It reminded me of the notices I'd sometimes see, placed around construction works: 'So-and-So By-Pass. X, Y and Z Construction. Design by Charles Bloggs, County Engineer.' No it wasn't. Bloggs may have got the committee to agree to it, and produce the funding, and he'll probably wear a sharp suit for the opening ceremony. But the design work was undertaken by a horde of knowledgeable and highly-qualified minions, and they don't get a mention anywhere. It's a bit like saying that George Stephenson built all the railways in Britain.

Our highways chief was also apt to take too much of an obsessive interest in what was going on with road-works, and was apt to stop alongside them, to the dismay – and sometimes terror – of the roads gangs, because his reason for stopping was not to congratulate them or to ask how things were going, but to criticise, admonish and do a lot of shouting. For that reason, his commuting route to work was always spick and span, and cleared early of snow. On one of his travels about the county he pulled up at a place where men were digging holes in the road and there were piles of materials and much use of bollards and barriers. He got out of his car, and shouted at one of the workers.

"Who's in charge here? Where's the foreman?"

The worker gesticulated towards another man in overalls,

who ambled over with a cigarette hanging from the corner of his mouth.

"Yeah?" asked the foreman.

The chief embarked on a loud tirade of complaint and critique. The site was untidy, the signing was atrocious, and so on and so on, and what were the public to make of it? The foreman listened, nodding gently, and when the diatribe had finished, took his cigarette from his mouth.

"Who are you, then?"

"My name's Halford," he barked, "and I'm the County Highways Engineer!"

The foreman looked him straight in the eye and said "Well we're the Electricity Board, so you can ferk off!" and he wandered back into the site to go about his business.

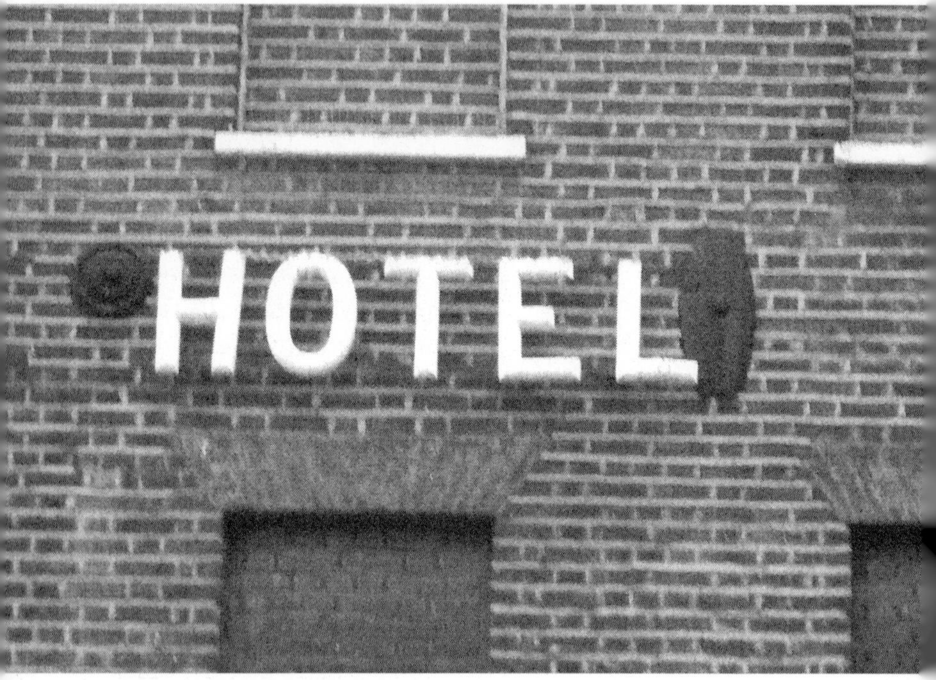
HOTEL

12

WHEN IN DOUBT, REORGANISE

L ondon's local government had been reorganised in the 1960s and there was a general feeling that this needed to happen in the rest of the country too. After all, local authorities had been set up to reflect society of the 1880s and 1890s and things had now changed beyond recognition.

So the government created a Royal Commission to review the situation. A cynical friend of mine once suggested that when a government couldn't make up its mind, or felt that it would be unpopular in making some decisions, it would set up a Royal Commission. The Commission would inevitably take a long time to report, and there was a good chance that when it did, the government who had set it up would be out of office, and it would appear to be all the fault of the new incumbents.

Something like this did indeed happen. There were various hefty reports with splendid maps which suggested doing away with counties, creating 'city regions', single tiers of administration and so on. Ted Heath's government decided to retain most of the existing counties and to invent a few new ones, such as Avon, that consisted of Bristol, Bath and their hinterlands; Humberside, which took in slices of Yorkshire and Lincolnshire; and Cleveland which was constituted from lumps of Yorkshire and County Durham. The new artificial counties attracted little love and loyalty, but that is another story. The counties were to look after the big jobs – highways, education, social services, and so on – and new district councils would manage the rest.

The New Jerusalem was to be in place on April Fools Day 1974. This meant eighteen months of scurrying around, setting up working parties and consultation groups. Masses of contemplation and planning took place, masterminded by serious-faced individuals in smoke-filled rooms. Every authority appointed groups of people to work out what the structure and duties of the new organisation should be: much of what came from these groups must at best have been an educated guess, and at worst nothing better than holding up a wet finger to determine the direction of the wind. Nevertheless, structure charts with job titles and grades attached to them sprouted like weeds, and various worthies must have made goodly sums of money from publishing books recommending how the new councils should function.

Eventually, jobs in the new organisations were advertised. For career (and salary) minded employees, it became bonanza time. There were plenty of old-style traditional jobs to perform, but also a raft of posts in new or expanded areas of expertise, such as Personnel. Existing employees could apply for any of the new jobs in any of the new authorities, but the remaining people were slotted into the more basic grade ones, many of which were practically unaltered.

Employees with particular skills were much in demand and people job-hopped with great vigour, often moving on before they had even started work because they'd found something else on an even higher salary. One bloke jumped from a middling clerical grade to that of principal officer by way of four posts on administrative, professional and senior officer grades without taking up any of the intermediate jobs he had been offered and which he had accepted.

With the new organisation, some jobs would simply be eliminated, such as the clerks and other chief officers of the old authorities. But they did pretty well out of it, too, negotiating favourable redundancy terms and enhanced pension arrangements, and then taking up positions on lower, but still lucrative, grades in the new councils.

And then there was something called 'Appendix E'. This was a system intended to ensure that people forcibly displaced from one location to another by reorganisation received payment for a number of years to compensate for the extra mileage. One of my colleagues applied of his own free will for a job in one of the new districts in another part of the county. He got the job, and because the new employer was desperate to fill the post, he successfully demanded 'Appendix E' payments for the extra sixty miles he'd have to drive every day.

As well as changes in people, there were changes in what the council did. At long last the Health Department was passed over to the NHS, where it always should have been, anyway. With the enormous expansion that was happening, the space at County Hall vacated by the health people was gratefully received. In spite of the fact that County Hall was relatively new, we had never really had enough room. This was partly due to the inexorable expansion of local government in the sixties and seventies, but it was also to the fact that when the building was in the planning stage, councillors had cross-questioned those responsible, including Vince, about which person or activity was to occupy each room. If the councillors received no firm information about occupation, they insisted that the room in question should be eliminated from the plans.

Some time before reorganisation Vince pleaded with the chief of the Health Department for him to remove a huge number of ancient files from the roof to allow the space to be occupied by more pressing items. The files in question were school medical and dental records going back to the late nineteenth century. The chief was adamant. Even though he admitted that the files were never looked at, and probably never would be, they could not be destroyed because people might want access to information about their, or their parents', youthful health. And that was that.

When the Health Department moved out of County Hall in early 1974, all the school medical and dental records were stacked on the loading bay ready for their mass removal a couple of days later.

By a curious quirk of fate, the bin men were on strike, and the rubbish from County Hall was piling up. When things were getting beyond a joke, the decision was made to ask the mechanical engineer's workshop to make an enormous wire basket which could be placed in a corner of the grounds and for the incineration of the paper rubbish from the offices. The cleaning team piled up the paperwork and two supervisors took it over to the basket where it was ceremoniously burnt.

On the day after the old health records had been stacked on the loading bay, we noticed that they had disappeared. I suggested to Vince that the removal was running ahead of schedule, but he disagreed, and made enquiries. He returned from his detective work with a broad grin on his face. The cleaning supervisors had, of course, mistaken the records for burnable rubbish, and had dealt with it accordingly. "Don't say a word; let's see what happens," said Vince.

Days turned into weeks, and weeks into months. No mention of the records was ever made, presumably because no-one had noticed their absence.

My contribution to the reorganisation came when I was asked to work on the recruitment and selection of staff. At that time I knew nothing about the process except what had happened to me when I applied for, and occasionally got, jobs, and, of course, I made every mistake in the book.

My allotted domain was the recruitment of clerical and secretarial people. Secretaries were extraordinarily difficult to come by, even though we offered slightly better pay and conditions than most other local employers, and because of the shortage of applicants we tended to be less rigorous about focusing on the real requirements for the work than we might have been. We thought, quite wrongly, that anybody would fit in and work all right, and as long as they passed a basic typing test they were welcomed in.

This lack of rigour occasionally backfired, and we became the home of some pretty awful new recruits. The conventional wisdom was that local government was a good employer, and being a good employer meant that you bent over backwards to avoid firing anyone: hence we had a problem. Poor staff affected the morale of the rest, and that meant we weren't a good employer at all. We did occasionally give people the elbow and my lax hiring criteria came back and bit me well and truly in the backside when I discovered that I had the job of getting rid of a couple of radical under-performers. One particularly sticks in my mind.

A department told me that the typist I had found for them was consistently late and when she did turn up, she was just not doing her job. She was also taking regular days off sick. Would I kindly get rid of her, please? I felt slightly aggrieved that they had chosen not to involve themselves in the process, which showed a distinct lack of bottle. Truth to tell, though, bottle was severely lacking on my part, too. No-one had really prepared me for recruiting people and certainly no-one had prepared me for firing them.

I was due to do the deed on a Friday, but the lady in question chose that day to go off sick, so the operation was postponed until the following Monday. I had a miserable weekend contemplating what I had to do, how I might go about doing it and what the reaction (tears, tantrums, temper, or all three of them) might be.

Monday eventually came. I sat nervously in my office as she breezed in, late of course, with a broad smile on her face. I cleared my throat and started.

"Thanks for coming to see me. I'll get straight to the point. I think there are a few little problems with the way you're working."

"I expect you'd like me to leave," she said with a broad smile. "I know I'm not that good and that I'm taking too much time off."

I was astounded. "Well, it's not that bad ..."

"Yes, it is," she said. "When do you want me to go?"

I was astonished at her innocent openness, and rather enjoyed her naive approach to the situation. I agreed that she should have a proper period of notice, and that we would concoct some form of reference which would support any future job applications she made (never trust references!). And that was the last I saw of her, although it wasn't the last I heard.

A couple of weeks later I was walking through the department she'd been employed in and I stopped to ask whether they knew if she'd landed another job.

"Not as far as I know, but she has had some interviews, though," my informant told me.

"She came back from one yesterday morning and at lunchtime confided in a colleague that she thought it was a bit weird. Apparently she had applied for a job which supposedly required secretarial skills, and was called for interview at" – here my informant mentioned a rather down market local hotel. "She went there, and was told that her interviewer, a Mr B, was to be found in room number 203. She was ushered into Mr B's room, where he told her about the job. Yes, there was a need for secretarial qualifications, but a great part of the work would be entertaining important foreign clients. Would she mind that? When she said 'no', the interviewer warmed to his theme and went on to suggest that he was only interested in employing people who were very presentable. With that in mind, would she mind taking off a few of her clothes so that he could see how she might match up? She had got down to the last two or three items before at long last it crossed her mind to wonder whether the interview was quite legitimate, so at this stage she made her apologies, got dressed and left. She asked the colleague in whom she was confiding if they thought she had done the right thing, and had not spoiled her chances of getting a really interesting job. The colleague said that Mr B sounded like a weirdo and persuaded her to ask me to phone the police."

The police duly pounced and bore off Mr B, who later appeared in court and then spent some time at Her Majesty's pleasure.

My approach to recruitment was not always appreciated by some of the Higher Ups. One of the ways in which I managed to irritate the more traditional chief officers was by ignoring a tome known colloquially as 'The Purple Book'. The proper title of this work was something like 'Terms and Conditions of Service for Local Government Employees in England and Wales': it was the bible of recruiters and had been originally published in the 1940s. It was undoubtedly complex enough when it was born, but with pages of detailed and often obscure updates added every year, it became virtually impenetrable even to experts. Very local government. Sadly for many, like a lot of manuals designed to help, it ceased to be a help and became a strait-jacket instead. One of the statements it contained was that to get a clerical job with a local authority, all candidates must have a minimum of five GCEs, including Mathematics and English.

Many of the basic-grade clerical jobs on offer, such filing or stuffing envelopes, were so straightforward that it seemed to me they hardly called for intellectual giants. In fact, people with even the basic educational requirements very often left quickly, bored out of their minds. I did not, therefore, toe the GCE line when it came to appointing people to this kind of work. I remember putting forward one young man who had left school with one or two rather poor CSEs, but who had a good attitude, for a potentially boring job in the finance department, and receiving a rocket from his section leader, who said that he would have to take the matter to his chief. Didn't I understand what The Purple Book said, and weren't the ratepayers entitled to have the very best people serving them? After a prolonged debate, I managed to persuade both section leader and chief that what mattered more for the job in question were the lad's approach and personal drive rather than his lack of formal qualifications, and they grudgingly allowed him to stay. "But we'll be keeping a firm eye on him during his probation period," the section leader offered as his parting comment.

Many years later I came across the fellow in question – no longer that young – again, and learned with pleasure that he had become a section leader himself. I felt rather pleased. It wasn't the pleasure of vindication, but was much more to do with an affirmation that in many cases attitude was just as, and sometimes more, important than paper qualifications.

One day we had an unannounced visit from a young woman enquiring if we had any secretarial vacancies. Though desperation for secretaries, we stopped short of tying her to the interviewee's chair, and airily suggested that we had one or two possible jobs. She took a typing test, and showed herself to be exceedingly competent. We offered her a job like a shot, and she seemed to be pleased to be able to join us. The only problem was that she was Swedish, and was staying in the UK on a student's visa which had only a few months to run.

She turned out to be a real star, and became a popular member of staff: her supervisor was adamant that she must be retained at all costs. We took up cudgels with the local Job Centre, with whom we had a pretty good working relationship, but they told us that visas were out of their hands. They also said that they felt that having a secretarial job would be unlikely to qualify her for a new visa, because the authorities usually felt a UK resident or someone from Commonwealth country was preferable. In vain did we argue that there weren't enough secretarial people to fill the vacancies in our area. "We don't make the rules," they said. 'We're only telling you what the rules are." And so it was that I learned that County Hall was not the only place where jobsworths could be found.

As I'm writing this (in 2012), the popular consensus is that Her Majesty's Home Office is currently somewhat dysfunctional. I must set the record straight and say that, in my perhaps somewhat limited experience, it always has been.

We eventually found a telephone number for the bowler hats in Whitehall: on many occasions over the following few days we either didn't get through or didn't get answered. Once or twice we did get a human voice which either put us through to someone else, who wasn't there, or who said that they couldn't help us and that we should get in touch with our local Job Centre or the passport office. We wrote letters which, for all we knew to the contrary, disappeared into a black hole somewhere in Whitehall because they were never replied to, and in the end we were forced to give up.

Sadly, we had to explain to our star that we had no option except to bid her farewell. She departed in tears for Scandinavia.

The day for regime change approached inexorably, with, it must be said, a measure of optimism for many, especially those who felt that they had done rather well in the impending re-organisation.

Not everyone was a winner. Some of the longer-established people found that their furrows were now being ploughed differently. One such was Keith Parsons, who I'd first met when I made my initial job overtures to the County Council. 'Establishment Officers' ceased to exist, being replaced by 'Personnel'. In spite of Keith's long experience and depth of knowledge, he lacked formal qualifications in 'Personnel', and he wasn't a member of the right professional institution, either, (in fact, he was probably not a member of *any* professional institution). First he was sidelined, and then forced to retire early. He was known to most in County Hall and his leaving presentation took place in a crowded committee room. After receiving whatever token of esteem had been collected for, he gave the traditional response of thanks, during which he sadly observed that he thought that the things he'd worked on over many years had gone pretty well, but after all his apparent good service, not only had they changed the game but they'd changed the rules – and omitted to tell him. It was a profoundly miserable experience to hear this gentle and much-loved man, a father-figure for some, mourn his passing with such restrained bitterness.

Apart from the departure of many old-timers, we acquired loads of new people to do new jobs. The bigger organisation would need a bigger systems team, a bigger O&M team – in fact, a bigger practically-any-kind of team. Our department was joined by a handful of statisticians and operational research men. What the latter got up to was largely a mystery to many of us, and, for all I know, to them, too, but two magnificently bald men were recruited to become the guardians of this arcane art. Their baldness was of passing interest because these were days well before the totally shaven head became fashionable, unless you were Yul Brynner. I formulated a theory that going bald might be due to wearing protective head-gear in rather extreme climates. One of the men in question had spent a long time as an army officer serving in Borneo where solar topees were *de rigueur*, and the other had spent a number of years as a number-crunching engineer on the construction of the Pacific Great Eastern Railway in the extreme north west of Canada where I fancied he must have worn a huge fur hat all winter.

The two were pretty soon farmed out to more appropriate parts of the council. The ex-pat Canadian went to the Highways Engineer, and Borneo man, Ralph, who we had nicknamed 'The Skull', went to the chief executive's policy advisory team, where he became involved in important crystal-gazing work.

On one occasion I needed to visit his office and found it empty, save for a fairly junior admin assistant who seemed on edge and distracted. After receiving a very short reply to my enquiry as to The Skull's whereabouts, and watching the junior assistant fidgeting uncomfortably in his seat for some seconds, I asked if anything was the matter.

"I really don't know what to do," he said miserably. "Ralph is in a meeting with the chief executive, a few more chief officers and some senior civil servants from some Ministry, and before he went in he instructed me that on no account, for any reason, should he be disturbed. I've just had a phone call from his wife, who insisted that he must come home very urgently, and I'm in a real dilemma."

"Did she say why she wanted him home?" I asked.

"Yes. His house is on fire."

I suggested that this might just be a good enough reason to interrupt the important meeting, and with obvious fear and trepidation the assistant knocked on the meeting room door and sidled in. Five seconds later he was propelled out backwards with some force as Ralph emerged as though from a rocket launcher and headed for the car park at a brisk run.

Getting ready for reorganisation caused some differences in the way elected councillors approached their work. Up to then party politics seldom penetrated the council chamber: for a long time we had been an 'Independent' council, although probably with a hidden tendency to being Conservative. In fact, for a number of years we had a chairman who, when welcoming those newly elected to the chamber, made a point of emphasising to them that the council was there for the good of the whole county, and that their party preferences, whatever they might be, should have little place in any deliberations.

All this changed as the election for the reorganised council approached. Political parties climbed on the bandwagon, and, knowing that many of the electorate would vote for almost anyone, provided they liked their political colour, told the sitting councillors, some of whom had served for years, that they should sign up with their party. If they didn't stand for the party, then the party would field someone else against them. A number of the stalwarts resisted. Some were duly defeated at election time, a few managed to retain their seats as independents, but the inevitable happened, and we became a party-political authority. Many of us felt that this was a sad day.

The nature of the people who became councillors changed too. Some might suggest that they became more 'professional', but I could never see this. I was at a loss to understand why the possession of a party membership card made them any more committed to the people they served. In fact, it probably made them less committed to those who didn't share their views about how the world should be run. Out went the enthusiastic amateur and the person who became a councillor because it was something to do with their time. We still retained a core of those solid and dedicated citizens who were committed to public service and who knew the system well. They were a great support, although were not shy of questioning those who carried out the work of the council. In addition, we acquired new councillors who were consistently confrontational, fiercely contesting every view or opinion of staff. Like most of us, I'd been around long enough to produce cogent, if not always totally convincing, arguments as to why things should progress in a particular way (this was a variation of the 'bullshit baffles brains' tactic). Occasionally the confrontational councillors had minor victories, and a pet scheme was shelved, or at least put on the back burner until we acquired a few more amenable councillors.

Less lucky were those who were elected because they vowed to cut costs. They very quickly found out that if you have a school, it needs staff and maintenance and a lot of other things, and if you have a road, it also needs maintaining and this requires workers. Room for financial manoeuvre was limited only to the occasional single percentage point of the budget, and this must have caused them great frustration. Unwittingly, they found themselves caught up with a gargantuan organisation with an inexhaustible financial appetite that went on its unstoppable way oblivious to any minor hiccups designed to stop its inexorable progress towards goodness-knows-what levels of expenditure.

Another type of elected representative which was on the increase was the poacher-turned-gamekeeper, a retired employee who stood for council. Reorganisation had meant that a number of quite senior people had been forced to take early retirement: having them return as councillors did cause a little concern to those

of us still on the payroll, because they knew the system. Using our time-honoured bullshit-baffles-brains techniques was no good because they saw straight through it. In another way, it was further evidence to support the notion that local government is a brilliantly self-perpetuating system.

Alongside the cost-cutting councillors were those elected on a 'single-issue' to represent a pressure group. You know the kind of thing. "I'm here to get a by-pass for the village of Little-Nothing-on-the-Wold, and I don't care about the other things that the council gets up to. I'll vote for the other things if I have to, but my only real interest is the by-pass." Many of these seemed quite surprised that they had to get involved in the Other Things, and their lack of interest in these must have been a real pain to other more committed people who sat on the same committees and *did* care about the council's work as a whole. Mind, the single-issue people haven't gone away. Only two or three years ago I was speaking to a very pleasant and long-serving county councillor, miles away from the one for which I used to work. "Of course I appreciate the importance of schools and highways and social services and so on," she said, "but what really matters to me is getting the dog poo off the streets of my town." I did wonder about her share in the governance of an organisation which in that financial year was due to spend well over six hundred million pounds.

The last few months of the old regime drifted past, and April Fools' Day arrived. I don't know quite what I was expecting, but there was a sense of anti-climax. No fireworks at midnight, no fanfares of trumpets or processions of the new heroes who were to govern the county. We didn't even move offices. There was a new letter-heading and a modern logo (well, sort of). And, of course, we assumed our new job titles, and, in many cases, including mine, the pay rises that went with them. Overnight, I received well over a thousand pounds more a year (a goodly sum in those days) for doing largely the same work as I had been doing on 31 March.

13

VINCE'S FLYING CIRCUS

All the fuss was more or less over and things were ticking over much as they had done before. The great growth in staff numbers ground to a halt, and with it the major purpose of my job. I won't say that the tap was turned off overnight, but recruitment reverted roughly to the level that it stood at before the reorganisation. A belated realisation had dawned in some quarters that some of the staff numbers claimed to be necessary for the new authority to function had been over-estimated. In fact, there was a surplus of bodies, but in true local government fashion these were soon found things to do and became firm parts of the fabric of the place. I'd come to expect this kind of thing in a business where supervisors' and managers' rewards were partly based upon the number of people in their teams. And anyway, the surplus bodies' salaries had been budgeted for, so that was all right, then.

Estimating how many staff would be needed in the new council was largely based on guesswork, and some departments realised pretty quickly that things weren't right. Attempts to iron out the difficulties were made by – guess what? – further mini-reorganisations. About this time, I realised that a key characteristic of public sector organisations is that, no matter what the problem, the answer is always to reorganise. Management structures and job titles are changed, sometimes several times, but usually reorganising only works in a limited way and never addresses the underlying issues.

With recruitment in sharp decline, whatever was to become of me? Good old Benign and Fatherly had not only retained his job, and gained a more important-sounding title, but had also significantly increased the size of his fiefdom, and I learned that he spent parts of his review meetings looking at his department's staffing and muttering "What are we going to do about Philips?"

Circumstances came to the rescue. Some years previously, as a spin-off from Harold Wilson's drive for the white heat of technology, Training Boards had been set up to encourage industry to enhance employee skills. These were a national government initiative for industry and commerce, but local authorities were certainly not going to be outdone, so they formed one of their own – the Local Government Training Board. It sat in Luton, and was partly funded by a levy made on every local authority based upon the number of people on their payrolls. As some recompense, the Board paid a grant to local authorities to cover the costs of staff training, which meant that if an authority was smart it could make a reasonably hefty profit on the deal. It also helped to fund a training officer in each authority.

The man appointed to our county council was Patrick Stephens, who knew every little dodge and tactic to get the best out of the Board – he had cut his teeth on it with another council in the north of England. He helped us get smart with the training money available, and for a number of years finance for anything that could remotely be called training was claimed from the coffers in Luton, and sucked into our budget.

A lot of old-stagers saw all this 'training nonsense' as a waste of time and money, an unnecessary frippery, or something that only happened if people had been naughty. Luckily Patrick, helped by the promise of cash from the Board, was able to persuade Benign and Fatherly and his management team that it was a useful activity as well as being fashionable, and after the successful persuasion protested that he couldn't do everything on his own. This probably coincided with one of the meetings when the mournful muttering of the "What are we going to do about Philips?" mantra took place, and as a result three of us who were getting a bit superfluous were gathered up to form the Training Team.

To my delight, one of the three was my mentor from former times, Vince, who was working his way gently towards early retirement. His knowledge of training came largely from his RAF experience in the war, where he had mentored newer and greener recruits. The second of the transferees was the deputy county ambulance officer who had had to relinquish his uniform when the job was transferred to the NHS. He became the first-aid training guru, quickly acquiring the nickname 'Bandage Bernie', and later looked after other aspects of health and safety training as well. Luckily, he did not entirely have to bid farewell to uniformed service: as an active member of the St John Ambulance Association, he was able to wear their livery whenever the occasion demanded. And then there was me: I had about as much knowledge of training as I'd previously had of staff recruitment when I was pressed into doing that, namely, very little.

By dint of persistence we acquired the use of a room in the bomb-proof dungeon, right next to the room designated as the potential nerve-centre for the conduct of our county's part in World War Three. The dungeon was not awfully conducive to relaxed learning, so we contrived to get some carpet squares laid, sought out some reasonably comfortable chairs and cajoled the maintenance people into painting the walls in light colours. We put shades on the glaring fluorescent tubes, and installed a drinks machine which dispensed beverages that largely tasted like death, but which had the advantage of being free. The place became a reasonably habitable training centre.

Patrick decided that the first and most urgent need was for Induction Training, something that was becoming very fashionable. The idea of induction is to familiarise new recruits with the aims of the business, the way it functions and maybe a little about its background. The thinking was that if they understood what it was all about, they would become useful and happy members of staff all the more quickly.

Vince and I scoured magazine articles and papers on the subject for clues, and phoned around a few people in other places to find out how they were doing it. Over a few days we got our own programme together, and decided to run a pilot Induction Course in our new training room. All departments were asked to send people along, and Vince, Patrick and myself shared out the topics to be covered. Bandage Bernie, rather surprisingly, did not want to include first aid as part of the course, despite the fact that this would have given him an opportunity to don his uniform. "Far too technical for junior newcomers," was his view. Vince and I may have been pretty ignorant about training techniques, but we were both involved in amateur dramatics, so we felt that we could make a fist of addressing the assembled masses. Patrick, though not a thespian, was used to flannelling and shooting the bull at high level and could therefore be expected to cope with speaking to the less exalted.

The day for the pilot arrived. Nervous delegates helped themselves to the deathly beverage of their choice, and sat in silence waiting for the action to begin. Off we went. Introductions, 'what local government does and how the county council works' got us going, even if it wasn't terribly exciting. 'Where the money comes from, and where it goes' followed somewhat unpromisingly, and by lunch time expressions had become glazed and what little concentration there had been was definitely wilting. "Never mind," we told our disconsolate audience. "This afternoon will be full of variety." We gave them all a voucher for a sandwich in the staff club (no expense spared, recharged to the Training Board), and sent them out into the fresh air.

The afternoon got under way. Some words about the importance of communication, discussion about dealing with the public, with those of us at the front of the room doing most of the discussing, and then some practice in writing a simple letter. After this we hit a stumbling block. When we were planning the day, it had seemed a splendid idea to invite all the departmental heads to introduce themselves to those in the room, and to speak for five minutes on the work of their various domains. This turned out to be a cardinal error. Giving these mighty people the opportunity to pontificate upon their importance was a grave mistake. All save one far exceeded their allotted time, and most turned out to be tedious. None of them, except the last man in, seemed in any way sensitive to their audience's boredom. The chap representing the Education Department even brought with him a stack of Acts of Parliament, which he assured everyone underpinned his every movement, and gave a resume of each, starting around 1872 with the work of the Gladstone government.

The saviour of the day was the County Planning Officer, who was keenly aware that it was well past the hour when most people usually left the building. He put on a blinding two-minute performance.

"I know it's late," he said, "but I have to tell you what my department does. We advise people about plans."

He picked up and brandished a roll of paper which he flattened out.

"This is a plan." He tilted his head, frowned slightly and said "Hm. Don't know what of, but it's definitely a plan. We also deal with planning applications which are sent in by people who want to put up new buildings, or make alterations."

At this point he produced a form, looked at it and waved it in the air. "This is a planning application. Ah, I see we turned this one down. But we do pass them sometimes. On occasions I am asked how we arrive at planning decisions. I have all sorts of clever people working for me who tell me that planning and making decisions about it is a very scientific business, but I have to tell you in confidence that I have a crystal ball locked in one of my filing cabinets, and it helps a bit."

After a couple more sentences, followed by courteous wishes for the future success of the no-longer-bored audience, he swept out of the room and the day ended.

We learned a lot from that first induction day (immediately eliminating the pontificating from the heads of departments) and lightened up the programme for subsequent events. In an attempt to leaven the contents a little, we got hold of a 16mm movie film produced by Monmouthshire County Council, and future groups were treated to twenty minutes of colour footage demonstrating what that council did, which was almost exactly what ours did, too.

We took the programme on the road around the county and for three months or so we were doing one or two induction sessions a week. Patrick didn't drive, so Vince and I took turns. Time after time we loaded our cars with flip charts, overhead projector, film projector, screen and heaps of information handouts, and set off for distant parts in the hope of informing and entertaining those who were enjoying their first months with the council. So regular were our appearances in some venues that we became known as

Vince's Flying Circus. It was good fun, but I came to detest the ageing projection screen, which seemed to have a life of its own. I quickly discovered that its favourite trick was to make all its folding parts move in such a way as to foul its passage, and mine, through double swing-doors. It was probably the most entertaining thing the audience saw.

At every induction, we had a list of names of attendees, but it was rarely accurate and we got used to extra people turning up unannounced. At one venue there was a knowledgeable and enthusiastic lady who we were not expecting in our audience. She seemed deeply involved with what we were trying to do, and made repeated and splendidly helpful references to the various topics. When we broke for lunch, she came over to us.

"Do you know, I have really enjoyed this morning and I learned a lot," she said.

"Thanks very much," said Vince. "It's nice to know we're on the right track with these induction programmes. How are you settling in at the council?

"Oh, I've been working in Social Services here for fifteen years. I came today expecting it to be a course on childcare legislation. I think I must have come on the wrong day."

Very often, as a reward to ourselves after an induction day, we would pack up our goods and chattels, tame the projection screen, and then head off somewhere for a drink and a meal. Because Patrick didn't drive he always made the most of the drink bit. After we had eaten, whoever was chauffeur for the day would indulge in some ostentatious examination of their watch, which Patrick would equally ostentatiously ignore.

My lack of real knowledge of training clearly had to be remedied. Because of the upsurge in training activity by local authorities, many tyros like me had been appointed, and the Training Board had tied up a deal with Sheffield Polytechnic to run 'train the trainer' programmes. These were available free of charge, and Patrick decided that we should have our share of the action. Vince was deemed too close to retirement for a burst of Sheffield, so the pleasure of the first visit fell to our sometimes uniformed friend, who duly departed for a fortnight in the north.

I was to have my burst a few weeks later, and I eagerly awaited our colleague's return so that I could learn what delights awaited me. After the fortnight he reappeared, angry and miserable.

"What was it like?"

"Utter bloody waste of time. All they did was talk about 'behaviour' and what made people tick. They didn't say a word about teaching. I was looking for some tips to confirm that I trained people well, and I didn't get any. I didn't learn anything. All feely-touchy pseudo-psychology. What good is that to me?"

The probable reason for this outburst was that Bandage Bernie trained people in what might be called the 'traditional style'. This meant the audience sat in serried ranks while they were told what to do, usually with the aid of blackboards and a pointer, the odd pre-prepared diagram and in the case of first aid training, a skeleton and a set of resuscitation dummies. The intimation of this method was that the person at the front was the expert and always knew best. It was 'training by numbers' and understanding the audience and their needs just didn't come into the equation at all.

I was intrigued by his comments because I suppose I too thought that effective training might be done by following some specific menu of approaches and activities. The 'menu' approach is still very much with us, and in my later training life, I came across many highly frustrated people who attended management courses and were disappointed that they didn't walk away with a laminated card upon which were listed a series of bullet points beneath the heading 'How to Manage'.

So I set off for Sheffield prepared to be disappointed, and returned two weeks later simply confused. Almost against my better judgement, I'd learned rather a lot.

Fifteen of us from various backgrounds and from across the country were thrown into the arms of the Polytechnic's Management School, which, in those days, occupied a row of rather nice Victorian terraced houses in a not unpleasant suburb of Sheffield called Totley. We were drawn from a number of local government disciplines. There were three or four social workers, a parks-and-gardens man just up off the tools, a couple of computer people, an engineer and, inevitably, a number of personnel types of which, I suppose, I was one.

We were all put up at a moderate hotel near the city centre. Because none of us really knew what to expect from the course, and all of us were a little dubious about the hotel, that we were very quickly gelled into a team that worked and played well together. The gelling began on the very first night when we were sitting at the table reserved for us in the hotel's restaurant. In the distance could be heard the Italian *maitre d'* instructing two or three of his lackeys, while gesticulating in our direction: "Don't-a waste too much time with them. They are from the Polytechnic, and they don't-a tip!" This seemed a perfect invitation to be slightly difficult, of which we took advantage for the whole fortnight. The *maitre d'* marginally got his own back on our last night, when we decided to push the boat out a little and moved, at our own expense, of course, to the *A La Carte* menu. The dinner was served with slightly more of a flourish than we had come to expect, perhaps in the expectation that there might be tips after all. A number chose steak Diane for the main course, which, frankly, disappointed. The *maitre d'* oiled his way around the table enquiring if everything was to our satisfaction.

"Actually, my steak is rather tough," one of the team had the temerity to say.

"What-a you expect? Steak-a Diane is always tough!" He snorted and stomped off huffily. His earlier prediction about tipping came true.

We were rather a motley gang, with a motley set of backgrounds, but through discussions in and out of the classroom we all learnt much about each other. I rather enjoyed hearing from one of the social workers, Dick, about things that happened while he was taking his social work qualifications. He had decided to enter the profession after a number of years as an engineer, not because he felt that he was an inadequate engineer, but because as the years passed he had become more interested in taking on a different kind of challenge. He lived near Hull, and went to a university which was close enough to allow him to return home to his family at weekends. After a while, one of his tutors thought it would be a good idea for the students to spend Monday mornings recounting to their colleagues what they'd done at the weekend and how they had dealt with difficulties and relationships.

Now, by his own admission, Dick's domestic life may not have been a paradise on earth, but it was pretty good. Every Monday morning, week after week, when it came to his turn in the soul-baring session, he would report that he had had a good weekend. His wife and children were pleased to see him when he arrived home on Friday night. The children talked to him about what they had done at school; on Saturday they all went shopping together, or visited friends or family; his garden was doing well, and things were generally harmonious. The other students may or may not have been envious of his apparent domestic comfort, but in social work terms he felt that it showed that a conventional family life could be pleasant and worthwhile.

A few weeks of this passed, and then on one occasion after the soul-bearing stint had been completed, his tutor asked him to have a chat after the class had finished.

"Look, Dick, I'll come straight to the point. Do you honestly believe that social work is for you?"

Dick started with amazement. "Of course I do. I gave up a well-paid job to do this course, and my heart is set on qualifying and practising as a social worker. Why do you ask? Isn't my course work good enough?"

"Oh, there is nothing at all wrong with your work, Dick. It's just that you don't seem to have enough stress in your personal life to understand the difficulties that many people encounter, and that might not help you in social work."

"I'm not sure where you're going with this," said Dick, unable to see the tutor's reasoning.

"Look for something, anything, in your own life about which you feel a bit nonplussed or uncomfortable," said the tutor.

And Dick, who really *did* want to become a social worker and who *did* have a pretty good domestic life, spent the rest of the term inventing little ripples in his domesticity with which to entertain the rest of the class on a Monday morning. The tutor was pleased that Dick had become more perceptive about the things that happened around him.

Also in our group were a couple of youngish married women who seemed to be having a few domestic problems. Not that they wore the problems on their sleeves, but from casual conversations there did seem to be things in their lives that were awry. If this was the case, I felt it was the men in their lives who must be lacking in something. The women seemed perfectly nice, and I wouldn't have hesitated to try domesticity with either of them, not that that would have been possible of course, since I was then newly married. Still, their relative openness about things would have stood them in good stead had they been student social workers at Dick's university!

One of our number was a local lad. He lived up the road in Barnsley, and was immensely proud of the town, and particularly its football club. At that time the club had shaken off any pretence of former glory, and was languishing in an unhealthy position in the fourth division of the English Football League, a fact that a few of us referred to whenever we thought our friend was waxing a little over-enthusiastic. Nevertheless, quite a crowd of us spent an enjoyable evening with him at the Barnsley Football Club Social Club, where we indulged in cheap beer and a different atmosphere from the Sheffield pubs. Our friend introduced us to a former Barnsley player, Skinner Normanton, who could be found in the Social Club on most nights. My previous knowledge of this retired local star was derived from reading fond comments about him in some of the regular articles in the *Observer* written by Michael Parkinson, himself a Barnsley man, who was a youthful watcher of Skinner's footballing skills. How tenuous are some of my claims to fame!

The course at the polytechnic wasn't hard work, but what was difficult was trying to relate the topics we discussed and exercises that we did to the real world of staff training. Marginally disturbing, too, was the business of giving and receiving honest feedback about how we felt and how we viewed situations and other people's attitudes. After all, most of us had spent some of our youth in the more formal 50s, when stiff upper lips ruled and open commentary about feelings was simply not on. Our tutors actually dictated very little to us about what were right or wrong techniques (which was exactly what had aggravated Bandage Bernie), and encouraged us to learn by discovery. For those of us seeking some kind of structure this was disconcerting.

Our tutors, too, let us dictate how things should go much of the time. The weather for our fortnight was sunny and warm, and one of the delights about the part of Sheffield that we were in was that it was only a few minutes' drive from the edge of the Peak District. Partly in the spirit of "trying it on" we suggested one afternoon that we should do the remainder of the day's work in the fresh air, at some picturesque location. Our tutors seemed quite happy to let this happen: off we went, and a good and relaxing afternoon it was, too. Of course, what the tutors were doing, cleverly, was enabling us, if we had a mind to, to understand the importance of enabling people who were learning to explore things for themselves, and maybe get a little enjoyment, as well as insight, on the way. I gradually came to appreciate this approach, and much later I discovered a line from *The Prophet* by Kahlil Gibran which summed it up better than I could ever have managed – "If a teacher is indeed wise he does not bid you enter the house of his wisdom, but rather leads you to the threshold of your own mind". I once tried this quote out on Bandage Bernie, but he replied sternly that it was all very fine, but wouldn't work for first aid.

The fortnight drew to a close, and it was time to go back to the office. Patrick took me aside during my first morning.

"I've heard mixed reports of the course," he said. "What did you make of it?"

"I think that mostly it was all right," I said. "I'm a bit confused about some of the stuff and I need time to get my thoughts in order."

"What did you learn?"

"Ask me again in about six months," I said, which he did. By this time one or two pennies had dropped, and my post-course review was quite positive.

We were soon in the thick of another couple of Flying Circuses which toured the county. This was the period when there was a burst of government legislation about employment and the workplace, and it was deemed that many people around the county needed to know what it meant for them. Although doubtless good stuff and probably necessary, employment law and health and safety practices at work were pretty mind-numbingly boring to present, especially to audiences with set views about what was necessary and what was right and wrong, anyway. These circuses were, therefore, not a lot of fun, unless you count odd argumentative exchanges of the "Listen, I've been using chain-saws for years, and if you think I'm going to wear all this protective clothing, safety boots, saw-proof jacket, gloves, goggles and ear defenders, especially on hot summer days, you've got another think coming!" variety. Interestingly, only a few years elapsed before those who made such statements would be loudly demanding all this kind of kit before they would even think about coming to work.

Once the statutory stuff was out of the way, we were able to start flexing our training muscles in some other directions. Management and supervisor training was becoming fashionable, so we leapt onto that bandwagon. In our naivety, we assumed that managers and supervisors would be queuing up to attend these training programmes, but this was not to be the case. Most frequently the reaction was:

"I've been a manager for twelve years, and I don't need to go on a course to tell me how to do it"

or:

"I'm the best-qualified architect in the department, and that automatically means I can manage well"

or:

"Are you telling me that I'm a bad manager?"

In the case of this last comment it was often extremely tempting to reply "Yes!", but, being well-mannered and tactful, we never did. It was sometimes an uphill struggle to persuade people to attend our extravaganzas on the off-chance that they might learn something useful, but some did come along to have their existing methods confirmed as brilliant.

In those days we knew little about management training, so we hired specialists to front the events for us until we had learned enough to do it for ourselves. A dilemma with which we were quickly faced was how long these sessions should last. There was a lot to get through – too much for a one-day programme – but in such a large county, managers would spend much of the time commuting back and forth. We decided the most sensible answer would be to run the programmes as residential courses. After all, this is what a lot of commercial concerns were doing, and there were undoubted advantages in giving people space and time-out from their workaday environments. But where to do it? We dared not use hotels because we were haunted by the prospect of uncomprehending questions being asked in committee, or newspaper headlines shouting about county council managers enjoying themselves at the rate-payers' expense.

Lady luck, or rather the vagaries of government policy, came to our rescue. Two or three years previously our police force had received considerable government funding to create a rather splendid training centre next to their headquarters. Its lecture and meeting rooms were state-of-the-art and it was surrounded by four or five residential blocks. The facilities were underused because although they began by offering cadet training as well as training for well-established members of the force, cadet funding was then withdrawn.

We heard about this, went to see the chief constable's men and were granted the use of some of the training and residential space at favourable rates for a year or two.

Because we were dealing with a disciplined organisation, the arrangements for our appearances at the training college went like clockwork, and we soon discovered that off-shoots of this discipline applied to us, too. The officer in charge of the centre suggested – nay, insisted – that a member of his staff should welcome our groups of participants, explain how the centre ran and outline the rules which applied to those using the place. This seemed like a good idea, and we readily agreed.

The first time we used the training centre, we were hosted by a pleasant, if a little formal, Inspector, who introduced himself to our gang, talked a little about the history and uses of the facility, and laid out the ground rules. I particularly enjoyed hearing the rules about the ashtrays, of which there were plenty in the meeting rooms and along the corridors. "It would be appreciated," he said, "if you could refrain from using the ashtrays, because the cleaners don't like dealing with them." Then there were the instructions about the catering arrangements: meal times and breaks for tea and coffee were tightly scheduled, and we were told to "please stick closely to the times. If you don't, the canteen staff will be unhappy." In spite of the number of uniformed officers, sporting sometimes amazing quantities of silver braid, who hovered around the place, I was tempted to wonder who was running things.

On one occasion our welcome was conducted by a slightly terrifying and solidly built policewoman sergeant. All the usual details were covered in her short speech, but she finished with a warning that we hadn't heard before. She gazed around the assembled company, which on this occasion consisted of largely middle-aged, world-weary males, fixed them with a beady eye and sternly informed them in John-Cleese-like tones that "It is an absolute rule that there will be no fraternising in the houses". From their demeanour, a gang less likely to fraternise in any way seemed hard to imagine.

One of the arguments we used to support our introduction of residential training was that we could run evening sessions after the break for dinner (or, as the constabulary called it, 'high tea'), thus creating extra hours of study. We later termed this as 'training by endurance', which wasn't necessarily a good idea, but to start with it swung the deal for us. One of the attractions of a residential course was the ability to relax at the day's end over a drink in the bar. To be sure, the police college had a bar, but because it was the police college, licensing hours were rigidly adhered to, and great was the frustration of some of our people when we had loquacious speakers for the after-dinner – or high tea – sessions. It fell to me to attract the eye (unostentatiously, of course) of these worthies at the appropriate time, and suggesting by sign language that they should wind up so we all had time for a pint or two. With a few of the more enthusiastic, I had to forget the subtlety and break my silence. Either way, the sighs of relief from the captive audience were almost audible.

One or two regular attenders, who had got to know the ropes and the rigours of closing time, used to bring the odd bottle with them for consumption in their rooms. Usually they invited a few chosen co-sufferers from the course to join them to share a glass. Whether this counted as fraternisation I wasn't sure.

At the age of 34 I still really didn't know what I wanted to do for a career, but in training, I had found something that I was not too bad at doing, and which was fun. It occupied the rest of my time in local government, and indeed much of the remainder of my working life. I hoped that I was no longer a jobsworth and could encourage others to break free too. The road to hell, of course, is paved with good intentions, and I knew that my enthusiasm for doing things differently would have cold water poured all over it once the delegates got back to their desks.

"Had a nice holiday?" their managers would ask. "Well, you're back in the real world now, so you can forget all that claptrap you've been listening to in the classroom!"

EPILOGUE

A year or two after the big 1974 reorganisation there was a bomb scare. A man telephoned and said that there was a bomb in County Hall and that it was timed to detonate at eleven o'clock in the morning.

Not for us, in those rather more naive days, the white heat of action we would expect today. No fleets of flashing blue lights or mass evacuations. No cordons or barriers or closures of adjacent roads. A policeman did amble over to talk to us. We were all informed of the state of affairs, told to look out for anything out of the ordinary, and to carry on as usual.

Eleven o'clock came and went. A little later I was walking down a quiet corridor and passed a colleague who was blessed with a dry Liverpudlian wit.

"Well that's eleven o'clock gone and nothing's happened," I said. "I suppose we all knew that it was probably a hoax."

He looked at me with a slightly pityingly straight face, shook his head and replied "But the bomb *did* go off, and this is paradise."

I eventually left public service, but from time to time continued to work with people from local authorities. Sometimes when trading tales and experiences with the old-stagers, one of them would observe sadly "Local government isn't what it used to be." I usually earnestly agreed with them: a lot of it didn't sound like fun any more. Then I remembered some of the attitudes and practices that had surrounded me during my time and a small internal voice muttered confidentially to me "Thank goodness!"

TOWN HALL

AFTERWORD

MORE THAN MY JOB'S WORTH

Historically, local government is largely all the fault of royalty, national governments and the church. These august bodies needed governable territories, and therefore created laws that would dictate how the populace lived. They also needed money to go to war, build great edifices and acquire luxury items such as chalices and cloth of gold: they raised the money for these through taxes and levies. The buildings and luxury goods were intended to make their lives more comfortable and to impress the hell out of the royalty and governments of other places, and, of course, God (interesting question: can one impress the hell out of God?).

Over time, their range of activities broadened, and they felt it would be a Good Thing to provide the populace with – for instance – education and social welfare. But as life became more complicated it was clear that a group of people sitting in the middle of the territory couldn't do everything (although today there are still Members of Parliament who think that they can), and over time responsibility for many public services was vested in local groups, such as parishes, who administered them for local people. Local government business continued to grow and grow, with other bodies like Poor Law Guardians and Justices of the Peace taking on bits of the action, and later a motley collection of Boards – School Boards, Burial Boards, Water Boards and the like – sprang up. Of course, just like today, no Board or group would talk to, or cooperate, with any other group and the result was chaos. In the latter part of the nineteenth century this was all swept away and replaced firstly by an administration based on the ancient counties and then eventually by more local councils looking after urban and rural areas.

The people who headed up these councils were drawn from that segment of society known as the Great and the Good, though many of them were probably neither every great nor very good. Increasingly, the voice of the people was heard and locals elected their own representatives to act as overseers of local affairs. These worthies decided what needed to be done and instructed the small number of paid officials to get on with it. The most powerful of these officials was the Clerk of the Council, usually a lawyer. This was handy because all local government activities were dictated by government statute or locally devised by-law, and lawyers have always made a pretty good living out of interpreting the words written down by other lawyers.

The need for services and the desire to provide them, expanded enormously over the years, and this meant that elected councillors needed more hired hands – technical experts, administrators to deal with the proliferation of forms and files, and practical people to mend roads, collect refuse, and look after parks and gardens.

So now throughout the kingdom there are large council offices full of hundreds of people spending their days doing incomprehensible things, watched over by worthies who claim to represent our hopes, needs and desires but often have no idea at all what's going on. And this complex system will doubtless continue *ad infinitum*. The halcyon days of local government were considered by many who worked for it to be the period of its seemingly inexorable growth during the 1960s and 70s, and it's surely no coincidence it was these decades which spawned the term Jobsworth.

When you work in a highly structured organisation, whose whole existence revolves around statutes and arcane bits of law, you get to be permanently mindful of the rules and become, almost without realising it, a Jobsworth. The *Oxford English Dictionary* defines a Jobsworth as "a person in authority, especially a minor official, who insists on adhering to rules and regulations or bureaucratic procedures even at the expense of common sense". It's a description I recognise only too well: during my time in local government we had more than our fair share of Jobsworths. I rather hope that I wasn't one of them, but then who am I to judge?